STARDUST

The Musings

of a

Gradually Awakening Soul

by Becca Zinn

This book is manufactured in the United States of
America. Design and cover art by Joel Sheer Associ-
ates and distribution by Stillpoint Publishing.

Stillpoint Publishing
Box 640, Meetinghouse Road
Walpole, NH 03608

Published simultaneously in Canada
by Fitzhenry and Whiteside Limited, Toronto.

ISBN # 0-913299-38-3

A JOINT
Uni★Sun/Stillpoint
BOOK

DEDICATION

To my father

CONTENTS

PREFACE

This is a story of one journey. The Great Atlas for Seekers contains thousands of maps detailing routes to the soul, routes to God. I found my map on page 7,630 of the Atlas. I describe to you that map, one small map among many, in hopes that my lessons along the Great Road might inspire you to dust off your hiking boots and to join those of us who quest.

INTRODUCTION

Stardust is the account of a young woman's journey from rebellious nihilism and atheism through a spiritual wakening to an—I almost want to say reborn—woman in touch with God and her own soul.

It is a story that we are beginning to hear more and more frequently, although most people would be afraid or embarrassed or regard their experiences as too personal to share with the world. The story is described in similar language in *The Way of the Peaceful Warrior* and many other books just recently available for the general public.

It is the story of events that would have been unthinkable a few decades ago but which recently have begun to occur to dozens, then hundreds, then thousands of people who are ready to grow and learn, to open their eyes, ears, and hearts, and to let go of illusions. It is the path you can choose. It will be arduous and scary, painful and lonesome at times, but it will lead to love and truth, understanding and compassion.

Becca's honesty, her occasional despair, her wish to give up—all are friendly reminders to other seekers that it is our choice and our choice only whether we decide to travel the path of light or the path of darkness. It has occurred to me many times during my own years of trials and tribulations that we have the free choice, but we need to choose wisely. It is the time of the true separation of the wheat from the chaff. The question is for you and for me: Do we have the faith and the trust to follow the path of love and love only, knowing that it will lead to God from the little sparkle of God within that we call our soul? That is the choice and the only choice we have to make.

Becca's book will help those who are in doubt about their own path. It will help them to understand that everybody—that is every soul—has its own longing to return to this source of love. If we just try to become honest again with ourselves, if we don't let fear, criticism, blame, and doubt cloud our awareness, then we are on the path.

Elisabeth Kübler-Ross
Headwaters, Virginia
March 1986

FOREWORD

I grew up in a small southern town in the 40's and 50's. My religious upbringing was traditionally WASP-ish. Through the fault of no one in particular, my religious experience consisted mainly of boredom, although it was spiced with occasional bursts of short-lived spiritual fervor. My older brother and I struggled together to transcend the emptiness of church services by singing all the hymns backward. It was enough of a challenge to keep us awake. My brother grew up to be a marvelous musician and now sings hymns every Sunday—frontward.

As soon as I left my parents' home I renounced everything I had been taught to think of as religion. The 60's were wonderful years to be in college for those of us who needed to rebel. I concluded during my first psychology course that Jesus was a paranoid schizophrenic. I readily joined the "God is Dead" movement of that era, deciding that His death was much easier to deal with than His aliveness. I also concluded that Richard Nixon was doing terrible things to our country and that the war in Vietnam was wrong. God, Jesus, and Richard Nixon were neatly filed away in the filing cabinet of my mind, lurking together behind the letter N for "Nonsense, Not acceptable, and No way!"

Rejecting God, Jesus, and Nixon left me ripe for rejecting anything and everything I could think of. It was the golden age of nihilism and atheism, so I eagerly jumped aboard those bandwagons, celebrating my liberation from the constraints of conventional WASP-ism with great enthusiasm. It didn't take long, however, for me to realize that I had confused the joys of nihilism with freedom from parental rule. As I adjusted to the freedoms of almost-adulthood, I felt less of a need to rebel. As a result, atheism became boring and nihilism lost its meaning.

I had decided when I was ten years old that I wanted to be a psychologist. I remained true to my childhood decision and entered graduate school. I had discovered the depths of the human psyche and the ego, and I assumed that mastery of the psyche would bring meaning and happiness into my life. For years psychology did bring me happiness as I stretched toward an understanding of people, their feelings, their pains, their joys, and their enormous capacity for growth. For years I openly professed psychology as my religion. I was young, I was learning, I was growing, and I thought I was free. There was still no room or need in my life for God.

In the few years that preceded the birth of this book, I experienced the most persistent and the most crippling emotional pain I had ever known. By that time both my husband and I were experienced clinical psychologists. Many of our friends and colleagues were outstanding psychotherapists, well trained in healing the pains of folks like me. I received the aid my friends gave to me, but my pain would not abate. I began to feel hungry for something more. Hunger gave way to starvation, and starvation turned into desperation. Twice in moments of screaming anguish I found myself calling to the God who I had assumed was dead. Twice I heard the words, "Be patient."

The God of my childhood felt disturbingly like Santa Claus, but it seemed that my childhood image was the best I could muster at the time. I knew I had to start somewhere, so I allowed my Santa God to return to my consciousness as a viable figure, a needed ally.

I wish I had known earlier about the Great Atlas for Seekers. I wish I had known that paths exist and teachers appear when students are ready. I wish I had known that there was a reason for my suffering and anguish. I didn't know—not until The Birthday.

PART ONE

CHAPTER ONE:

THE BIRTHDAY

The day was a dull and grey one. I awoke with unsettled feelings in me and around me. I felt death in the air. Since I did not yet know my soul, there was no one to turn to, no one to ask the questions which had no answers. During my long run in the early morning drizzle, I looked into the gathering storm clouds, feeling an odd and unfamiliar identity with their power. The thought repeatedly came to my mind, "I suppose this would be as good a day as any to die."

Thoughts of death were not new or surprising to me. My father lay in bed two hundred miles away with dozens of tumors ticking like slow but inevitable time bombs in his brain. "Why not today?" I thought.

I finished my run, showered, and went into my office. On that morning I met with two psychotherapy clients before the phone call came. My mother's voice was clear, her words were simple. "It has begun," she said. The coma that we had watched for daily, the coma that we had known existed in our futures—it was here. Now. The journey was beginning now.

"Please, God, let him be alive when I get there," I prayed as I began the trek homeward. I wasn't sure why I wished so strongly to see my father lying in a coma, but my voice called into the skies hoping to be heard. "Let him be alive!"

When I saw Dad his eyes were closed, yet he seemed strangely not asleep. I knew very little about life after death. In the preceding few years I had renounced my earlier nihilist philosophy of birth-life-death-rot, but I did not yet know the alternative to rotting. I did not yet know souls. It was fortunate that I possessed a vague and abstract belief in the concept of the human soul, since that very little bit of belief provided me some comfort in what I knew were Dad's last hours.

Years earlier I had read medical studies indicating that coma victims can often hear what is said to them. With trust in that scientific data and with a vague sense that something special was in the air, I spoke to my dying father. I held his nearly lifeless head in my arms and whispered into his ear, expressing my gratitude for his love and kindness. I thanked him for fathering me and for the many special gifts he had contributed to my life. I knew I was saying my goodbyes, and the psychologist in me knew I was "finishing business." What I did not yet know was how clearly my soul and his were speaking in those final moments. We spoke perhaps more clearly than we had ever spoken in "real" life. He heard my soft goodbyes, he felt my tears on his cheek, he heard my wishing him a safe and glorious journey. But all that would not be clear to me for several more hours.

My father died that evening at home, lying in a familiar and comfortable room. He was surrounded by his family, a few dear friends, and our helpmates from the local hospice. I stroked his body and held his right hand as he took his last breath. "Adieu, sweet Daddy. Adieu."

My head dropped onto his right arm. Two intense flashes of yellow light shot through my closed eyes, and a feeling of profound peacefulness filled the room. The peacefulness was not an absence of pain. It was not relief that the drama was over. It was a presence, an almost tangible presence in the air which emitted an almost palpable warmth.

The warmth lingered in the air for the entire hour that Dad's body remained with us. We all returned to his bedside many times, stroking his hands, holding him, and saying our last goodbyes.

***   ***   ***   ***   ***   ***   ***

The morning was slow in arriving. The darkness of the night felt frightening, almost unbearable in its relentlessness. I awaited daybreak as though it held some relief from a very long and deep pain. The first rays of light found me running again and thinking of Dad. I ran a course that he and I had run together many times. I conversed with him in my mind, thanking him repeatedly for the very gentle way in which he had introduced me to death. "You were my first *real* death, Dad, my virgin voyage into an unknown land. Even now, just ten hours later, I feel richer and wiser. I don't understand why I feel this way, but I thank you."

I talked on and on, thanking him for the many loving moments we had shared during the past months and expressing my hopes that his journey had gone well. I told him I was very concerned about how he was doing and I deeply hoped he was happy. I talked with him about how I had felt at the moment of his death. As I spoke intimately with him in my mind, I was totally unaware of the power I was invoking. I did not yet realize the realness of my wishes, the creative potential in my thoughts, or the power of my love.

After a while I hesitated, unsure whether or not it was fair, or even sane, to be talking to him. Was I breaking some sacred rule? Was I engaging in some sort of cosmic or spiritual no-no? If there were no such thing as a soul that survives death, was I indulging in a psychologically risky form of wishful thinking by carrying on this conversation with my dead father? And if there were such a thing as a soul, was I bothering Dad or distracting him from far more important tasks? I began to doubt myself. In resignation, I issued an invitation for Dad to come run with me if he wished. Then I vowed to respect his heavenly privacy and to leave him alone.

I ran. I worked up a good pulse and a good sweat. My breathing was steady and even, my pulse comfortably high. Moments later I felt a gentle push against my left shoulder. As I turned around to see who was there, my life changed. As I turned around, I might as well have been dying—or being born. Every cell in my body vibrated with an energy I had never before known. Every sense was jolted into a new dimension of awareness. In one instant all questions had answers, all life made sense, and God was real. In one moment on one sunny morning, my life was changed and would never again be the same.

In front of me stood life eternal.

My father's spirit appeared before me as a soft, translucent mist. I had not yet read accounts of people who have had near-death experiences, and I was later amazed when their words described exactly what I saw. His spirit body floated slightly above the ground. He had a definite and recognizable form, yet there were no human features as such. His eyes were pure white light.

My father greeted me with a kind of love that can be described only with words like white, radiant, showering, and overwhelming. I felt as if my body were levitating above the ground and as though a high voltage electrical current shot through me. For a few moments—I know not how many—I was frozen in awe. Then he spoke.

His words came as clearly as if they were spoken aloud, but I did not hear them with my ears. His words were transmitted through my forehead, directly into my mind. I felt the words enter my mind and I heard them clearly, but my ears were not involved.

Dad's words answered all my silent and unspoken concerns. As he spoke I realized he had heard my questions and the conversation I was having with him as I ran. He assured me: "I am fine. My journey was safe and beautiful. I am very fine. I send love to all of you. Don't be scared, and don't hesitate to call me. I can be totally in my heavenly experience and totally with you at the same time."

The energy surging through me was so powerful that I physically hurt. It was like the sweet pain of ecstasy magnified a hundred times. I had to resume my running to dissipate its intensity. As I ran, my sobs and laughter were mixed with gasps of "Oh, my God!"

I could no longer visually see my father, but I could sense his presence, even his exact location. I saw fuzzy white splotches in the air that I called energy fields. As I ran through them, I felt showered by lights that made every inch of my skin tingle. I saw visions that were not "real," and I heard voices when no one was near. I felt invisible loving hands on my shoulders and soft touches against my cheeks.

For over an hour I was enraptured by my experiences. I did not pause to question or analyze. I simply floated in the sense of rapture, feeling the most profound peace and ecstasy I had ever known.

Before long "reality" interrupted my bliss, intruding in its typically abrasive and unsympathetic manner. Alongside reality walked a sobering voice which said, "Excuse me, but since you are a clinical psychologist, I thought you might be interested in checking the data here. You are actively hallucinating."

"Keen observation," I replied. "I noticed."

"Well," said the voice, "you might be flipping out or you might be flipping in. Either way, this hallucination stuff is serious business."

"I know. I know," I said. "Just leave me alone for now. I'll analyze it later."

I had never felt such power. I had never seen, felt, and heard things that gave my life such a clear sense of meaning. Crazy or not, I was determined to follow this new energy. No matter where it might lead, I was determined to follow.

***   ***   ***   ***   ***   ***   ***

During the two days before Dad's funeral and for several days afterward, I continued to experience loving hallucinations. I was on a cosmic, spiritual high. At the time I thought I had found Nirvana, so I was surprised when I crashed. It had not yet occurred to me that I was still in a human body, and, by definition, was not floating around in lovely pink and yellow ethers like Dad. At least not full time. Real life was ushered back in by my all-too-familiar Voice of Doubt. My frequent traveling companion in this great journey spoke to me, saying . . .

Logical Mind Voice of Doubt: This is all very touching and even clinically interesting. However, as a licensed psychologist in the state of North Carolina, you surely realize that what you have been experiencing is simply a series of stress-induced hallucinations. It is acceptable that you enjoy these hallucinations for a while if you wish. After all, they might help you in getting over the stress and grief of your father's death. But you must be careful not to take these experiences too seriously.

Becca: You overlook the fact that Dad's death was not terribly stressful to me. Not in the usual sense, anyway. Even before the morning after, his dying was a series of loving encounters and little miracles.

Voice of Doubt: We have a name for this type of ideation. It is called denial. In fact, I would call it massive denial. It seems that your father's death has driven you temporarily crazy.

Becca: I don't think so. What I'm feeling right now doesn't feel like crazy. I've tasted crazy before, and this isn't it.

Voice of Doubt: A word of advice—you had better stop this nonsense while you're only *temporarily* crazy.

Becca: *I saw him!* I saw him, felt him, and heard him. Even you, Voice of Doubt, even *you* have trouble doubting that one.

Voice of Doubt (reluctantly): True. But I'm working on it. Don't get too confident. I'm working on it.

*** *** *** *** *** *** ***

Voice of Doubt worked overtime in its attempts to return me to the mental condition I would have previously called sanity. Despite its warnings, threats, fear tactics, and name calling, my mind kept drifting back to the weeks and months that preceded Dad' s death. I felt compelled to undertake a review of the process of Dad's dying, as though there were important answers and long sought solutions dwelling there.

The more deeply I delved into my review, the more clearly I saw that Dad's journey toward death had been a profoundly liberating experience for him. As his brain decayed he was miraculously free from pain, so he had needed no sedatives or pain killers. His illness progressed rapidly. As it did, he possessed less and less of a brain, yet his "mind" was clear and free. As I remembered the journey we shared during those months, I began to see glimpses of the miracle of liberation, clues into the mystery of death, hints as to the meaning of the soul.

As the tumors grew over those painful and precious six months, Dad's consciousness seemed to be cleansed of all unnatural, unnecessary, encrusted bits of his old self. All excesses fell away and all spiritual malignancies died. His love shone brightly while his words lessened, his bodily functions deteriorated, and his brain decayed. The closer he came to physical death, the more he seemed to be a liberated being, a disembodied light. As I looked back I began to see. During those six months I had seen the promise of Spirit evolve right in front of my eyes. *I had watched my father become his soul!* For a few short months I had been a student, sitting and learning at the feet of a rapidly awakening soul.

Memories flooded my mind. One particularly poignant experience occurred a few weeks before Dad's death when a group of twenty of his former employees came to the house to visit him. By that point in his illness Dad could speak a few simple sentences, but his phrases were often scrambled and sometimes barely coherent. He spoke simply to his visitors, greeting them warmly but with few words. As the group of well-wishers prepared to leave, Dad began to speak. His words were hesitating and faltering. My mother and I looked at each other with shared apprehension that he might fail terribly at speech-making, causing himself unnecessary embarrassment.

I knew that Dad's guests would understand his frailty, but Dad was a proud and loquacious man. As he began to speak, however, I felt my fear and tension give way to relaxation. Something was happening. I did not know what it was, but I knew that something important was happening. He said, eloquently:

"I remember all of the years we have spent together in this business. I remember all of the years. I remember the wood, the nails, the fabric, the pieces of finished furniture. But in those years that we worked, we were not just making furniture. We were making friends. What I remember most is not the wood, not the furniture. What I remember most is the people. I remember you."

His guests left with tears in their eyes but with no awareness that they had just witnessed a miracle. I knew on that day that Dad's brain could not have made that speech. I vaguely sensed that someone else—someone somewhere, somehow—had given him those words.

***   ***   ***   ***   ***   ***   ***

My recollections of the six-month journey continued to teach me. The memories acted like rays of morning sun touching the fat buds of a daylily. Something inside me began to open. Something inside me began to look upward into the rays of the sun.

I remembered the last moments I had spent with my father while he still possessed what I used to think of as consciousness. I had been visiting at my parents' home, as I had done regularly during Dad's illness. As I was preparing to leave, I went into his room to say goodbye. I sat beside the bed, stroked Dad's head, and told him I would see him again soon. He was very tired and his mouth failed him when he tried to speak. He gazed deeply into my eyes and then gently patted the side of his bed. I did not understand and I did not respond. His gaze intensified. Again he gently patted the bed.

I remembered feeling a tingly sensation in my forehead and suddenly knowing what it was he was telling me. It was almost as though he spoke aloud to me, though he said no words. Dad invited me, beckoned me, urged me to cuddle close to him for what he surely knew would be the last time. I crawled into bed beside him and held him in my arms. He had no strength with which to hold me, so I held him. I cradled him and cuddled him just as he had done hundreds of times with me.

As I left his bedside I returned his loving gaze. My last words to him were, "I love you, Dad. You know that." It was the next day that I received my mother's call saying, "It has begun."

*** *** *** *** *** *** ***

As I struggled to silence the persistent, cynical mutterings of my Voice of Doubt and as I allowed my memories to teach me, I began to see many things more and more clearly—things that made less and less sense in terms of what I had always assumed was reality. I could see that in Dad's weakest hour, he was his strongest. With no functional brain, he was his wisest. With an increasingly useless body, he exuded wondrous amounts of love. None of the miracles and wonders of his dying made any sense to my logical mind, none was explainable in terms of any psychological theory I had ever learned, and none

cut the mustard whatsoever with my Voice of Doubt. Nevertheless, these inexplicable wonders were beckoning to me to experience them and to learn from them.

During the course of his dying, my father had taken my
hand and led me to the door of a new reality. He had not simply shown me how to cope creatively with the stresses of death
and dying. In fact, he had taught me nothing about coping. He
had shown me, instead, a glimpse of a new world.

That new world seemed to contain within it the antidote to
all the venoms I had ever known or feared. I longed to know
more of it. I longed to live in that world.

***   ***   ***   ***   ***   ***   ***

The days passed. Life returned to normal, or so it would have
appeared to someone standing outside my mind. Inside my
mind, everything was new. Old assumptions were shattered.
New hopes and possibilities appeared everywhere like seed-
lings sprouting in a summer garden. My mind was over-
whelmed with possibilities but fraught with uncertainty. I was
hungry for learnings, for insights, and for more contact with
Dad. I was filled with enthusiasm, yet there was so much that
I did not know. I had no plan, no map, no guidelines, and no
teacher. In short, I had no idea what I was doing.

I made an innocent mistake, one born of naiveté and excitement. I made the mistake of expecting that one marvelous,
fantastic, glorious, God-given miracle could contain all the
answers and just might give me the once-in-a-millenium opportunity to avoid learning life the hard way.

I was not spared. Truth did not leap into my mind. Wisdom
did not materialize in front of my eyes begging admission into
my consciousness. Naked baby angels did not descend from
the heavens blowing trumpets and heralding the arrival of
my enlightenment.

I felt mildly offended that I was not exempted from the hard
way. After all, I had seen a dead person floating in the air. I
had even talked with him! Didn't that give me some sort of
privilege, some kind of cosmic credit card? Apparently not.

It was already clear to me, although I was reluctant to admit it. In the innermost recesses of my heart I knew: If it is an easy life you want, stay away from spiritual endeavors. If it is an easy life you want, stay away from dead folks.

***　　***　　***　　***　　***　　***　　***

I had a very full week of psychotherapy appointments on my calender. And my other business, a landscape nursery, was demanding a lot of my time as we approached a busy fall season. I needed time to follow my new path, but I didn't seem to be stumbling upon either the time or the methods for instant enlightenment. Life, indeed, seemed hard.

I greeted my 10:00 therapy client, a woman I had known for many years. She consulted me occasionally for advice, but our relationship had become more a trusting friendship than a doctor-patient relationship. As she sat down she asked, "How is your father?"

I took a deep breath and managed to say the words calmly, "He died three weeks ago."

She sat very still, looking at me with slightly glazed but loving eyes. "I'm not surprised," she said. "This morning I was meditating when a new voice came to me. He said he is your father, and he asked me to help you."

Before I could respond, Voice of Doubt had intruded into my thoughts and threatened to make a mockery of Susan's gift.

Voice of Doubt: Well, Doctor Zinn, this is certainly an interesting twist! Imagine this one written up in a highbrow psychology journal: "Patient speaks to therapist's dead father and comes to therapy appointment to therapize the therapist." I am sure this would be received very warmly and openly by the professional community. And, if you're really lucky, it might even make the *National Enquirer.*

Becca: Take a sabbatical, Voice. Susan is a trained psychic counselor. Give her a chance.

Voice of Doubt: Now, listen to me! This infatuation with weirdness is going entirely too far.

Becca: I'll tell you what, Voice. You go on vacation for a few days. I'll listen to what Susan has to say. I'll be very scientific about this, suspending judgment until the data are in. When you come back from vacation, we'll discuss it. Deal?

Voice of Doubt: No deal. I'll hang around.

***   ***   ***   ***   ***   ***   ***

Several days later Susan and I sat comfortably on the floor and relaxed ourselves into light hypnotic trances. Susan instructed me to think as clearly as I could of Dad and to send thoughts of love to his soul. As I remembered special times and tender moments with Dad, the love inside me built into a vibrating pressure in my throat, my chest, and my head.

Susan began to report images that were coming to her mind. The types of images that she experienced are often referred to as trivia in the psychic trade. Susan's hit rate on the trivia was remarkably high. She correctly described my father's build and his physical features. She described the location where his soul had appeared to me, the site of many happy childhood memories with my Dad, and the star that shines brightly during the Christmas season atop the tallest mountain in my home town.

The purpose of the trivia was simply to assure us earthlings that we were talking to the right dead person. Once we were assured, the trivia ceased and the non-trivia began.

Dad's messages to me, channeled through Susan, were simple, loving, and comforting. He assured me of his love, his presence, and his willingness to help me. At the end of our visit, Susan asked if there were any questions I would like to ask my father. I asked for his continued guidance and support. Then, unsure whether or not this type of request were appropriate, I asked if he could help me find a very special necklace I had lost.

Susan took a slow, deep breath and focused her mind. She began to see steps leading up some stairs. Then she saw a bathroom sink with pipes underneath. She assured me that the necklace had not gone down the sink, but seemed somehow to be under the sink. She began to see something made of wood. "It seems circular," she said, "like a canister or box of some kind."

I knew of a small wooden box to which she might be referring. But why it would be in the upstairs bathroom cabinet and why my necklace would be in it, I did not know.

As we finished our session I felt tearfully happy. When I returned home later in the day I remembered Dad's information about the necklace. I walked upstairs with curiosity but with little expectation that what Susan had seen was true. I was so filled with love from our session that the psychic prediction hardly mattered.

As I opened the cabinet I was stunned. The wooden box was there. I reached for it with trembling hands. As I opened it my eyes fell upon a symbol of my father's love and his continued presence in my life. It was a symbol too powerful, too real for Voice of Doubt to refute. My necklace was there.

*** *** *** *** *** *** ***

I was an eager student. I ran every day, looking for those fuzzy white energy fields and asking for guidance. I meditated, I hypnotized myself, I talked to clouds, and I prayed. I began to pay very close attention to the voices rumbling around in my head. Slowly I became capable of differentiating the cast of characters who frequented my thoughts. I could easily hear my Voice of Doubt. From my years of psycho-training I could already identify my own childlike voice, my inner nurturer, and my cool and rational analyst. Over time and with Susan's help, I began to be able to do what no school of psychotherapy had ever taught me. I learned to tell the difference between thoughts generated within my own skull and those that came from other souls. Slowly, very slowly, I began to hear Dad as he spoke to me. His "voice" was clear, distinct, and uniquely his own. I talked with Dad, I dreamed of him, I invited him into my thoughts and into my everyday activities.

One day as I was meditating, I began to feel a strong tingling in my left hand. The more I told my hand to relax, the more it tingled. My hand, almost as though it were separate from my body and from my will, reached for a pen and began to write the words that softly entered my mind:

"My love to you. I'm here, baby. I'll help. No more pain for you. Let go of the pain. This is the truth: *God is.* Believe.

Sweet baby, remember me. What I have given you is only 1/100th of the light."

As I read these words, I felt a wave of the profound peacefulness I had come to treasure. As I basked in its warmth, I suddenly realized that throughout my life no one had ever called me baby—no one, that is, except Dad.

*** *** *** *** *** *** ***

When I was in graduate school I was taught that hallucinations are not good. In my work with the inpatients who inhabited the dark halls of the state hospital where I once worked, I enforced the rules that I had been taught. All hallucinations were considered to be smudges on the patient's ego record. If the diagnostician could gather enough data and substantiate enough hallucinations, then he or she was thoroughly justified in stamping CRAZY in red ink on the patient's forehead. In the world of mutually-agreed-upon reality, hallucinations are not nice.

Little did I know back then that in a few years I would be welcoming hallucinations with open arms. Little did I know back then that in a few years I would be spending tender moments and precious hours, day in and day out, conversing with dead people.

Voice of Doubt: Where is that red ink pad? This lady is nuts!

Becca: Maybe so. However, your argument overlooks the fact that my life now has meaning in places where none existed before. What do you say to that tidbit of information?

Voice of Doubt: Meaning! Ha! Don't talk to me about meaning. Any fool devoted to a cause can create "meaning" out of yesterday's garbage.

Becca: Right. I forgot myself for a moment. I was indulging in self-righteousness. The fact that you are a jerk does not justify my self-righteousness. There I go again. I keep losing my temper with you.

Voice of Doubt: If it were only your temper you were losing, I'd be quite relieved.

Becca: Listen, Voice. Whatever it is that you have done for me in the past and however it is that you have protected me, I thank you. I don't expect you to resign your job overnight. But

I must tell you, you're fired. I don't know what I will do without you when I need a bit of doubt, but I'll find a way.

Voice of Doubt: You'll be sorry for this.

Becca: I may. I really may. But I'll risk it.

***　　***　　***　　***　　***　　***　　***

Voice of Doubt did not resign. It plagued me with the perverted loyalty of an abusive lover. Every time I felt enthralled, it tried to pull me down. Every time I saw sparkling lights, it brought clouds of darkness. I escaped its determined clutches only in moments of prayer and meditation. Voice of Doubt held no power over me when I lifted myself into the realm of trust and faith.

My closeness to Dad's soul grew more and more comfortable, and hearing his words became easier and more gently reliable. In his dying Dad had given me a glimpse of a new world, a new reality. Now he seemed to be urging me to explore that new reality, to study its truths. And he was clearly offering to guide me with his love.

As he led me toward new realms, his comfort and reassurances were gentle. One day he quietly spoke these words inside my mind as my hand wrote:

"As I write to you, relax. Peace be unto you, baby. All is healing in you. Thus your tears. They flow like rain for daffodils. Your flowers have begun to grow after a long winter. I will be with you always.

"Only as you grow taller will the path be clear. But paths of light are always better than ones of darkness, no matter how well known and well lit is the darkness. Only through walking on will you see that you've been here all along. Your inner knowledge is clear. Only by listening to it can you hear me. I'm so glad to be here with you. So glad.

"No more pain, baby. No more tears of the cage. Be uncaged. Let me write for you words of peace, of memories. Remember me tossing you into the air? Remember how you swam like my little fish? Let us again eat watermelons in the grass and spit the seeds. I'm here as I always am. Let me take your hand. Let me comfort you. As you held me in my death, so am I always holding you in my heart."

CHAPTER TWO:

THE QUEST FOR MIRACLES

My new experiences and learnings were thrilling to me. I approached my journey the way a starving man approaches a banquet table. I asked for more and more and more. I asked for signs, for visions, for writings, for insights, for dreams. I asked for miracles great and small. I had already been given a grand miracle or two, but I wanted more. And more I got! Little miracles poured into my life like sunlight streaming through a window. Miracles were everywhere. They occurred with the intensity that was necessary to overshadow my all-too-persistent Voice of Doubt. They occurred with the regularity that was necessary to prevent me from falling into despair. My little miracles became signs to me that I was being led toward a fountain of understanding greater than anything I'd ever imagined.

My miracles became my best friends. They infused my life with a vibrancy that felt very akin to being in love. I cherish the scrapbook in which my miracle memories live. As I write of them, I make no attempts to insist upon their authenticity or to prove their validity. I offer them in the same ways they came to me. Miracles are like benches along the path, spots for the weary traveller to sit and rest. Miracles are like rays of sun breaking through storm clouds, gentle reminders of the Light that lives beyond our visual limits. Miracles are like spiritual amphetamines, causing one's energy to race with cosmic abandon and giving a taste of the power that must lie at the source of those miracles. I offer my miracles in the same way they were given to me—as tangible little gifts from the beneficent beyond.

***   ***   ***   ***   ***   ***   ***

Both of my parents had photographs of themselves taken soon after the tumors were discovered in Dad's brain. In the photograph of Dad that I chose, he looks the way I will always remember him—robust, playful, and kind. After his death I often gazed at that portrait, remembering him and recalling our times together. Once as I was gazing at the picture and conversing with Dad, my love for him was unusually clear and intense. I could literally feel warmth emitting from my body, particularly from my chest and my face, as I looked at his picture. Suddenly the eyes in the photograph became alive! Dad's eyes looked out of his portrait with an enlivened sparkle, and they moved to meet my astonished gaze as they exuded the warmth of shared love.

As soon as I felt consciously stunned by the oddness of what was happening, the portrait became only a picture on a piece of paper again. Miracles seem to be like that, recoiling from the glare of a critically analyzing ego. Who can blame them?

For months afterward I could repeat the experience any time I would allow myself to relax into a state of trusting calm and send to him all the love I felt. His eyes became a spiritual biofeedback machine for me, as they always reflected the depth of the love that I projected to him. His eyes came alive only when my love for him was simple, uncluttered, and powerfully clear. I learned quite inadvertently one of the primary lessons taught by the Spirit world. Our tuition for their lessons is love. Love is the only payment they ask, but they do expect us to pay love. Lots of love.

***   ***   ***   ***   ***   ***   ***

The voice that I used to call my trained intuition began to speak much more loudly during psychotherapy sessions. It became hard to ignore, even when I tried. One day the voice began repeating a name over and over again. "Margaret M.,

Margaret M., Margaret M.," it said.

I had no idea who Margaret M. was, and I didn't particularly care. I assumed I was simply bored and my mind was wandering onto irrelevant thoughts, so I tried to hush the Margaret M. nonsense and return my attention to my client's words. It didn't work.

A few minutes later my client mentioned fears and curiosities she had about death. She had never mentioned these feelings before. Since I had recently become intensely interested in the subject of death, my ears perked up. I asked if she had experienced the death of someone extremely close to her. She reported that the only significant death during her lifetime had been that of her adored grandmother.

I knew the subject was important—my internal therapist's meter of what is important and what is not told me that much. I felt something different, though, something like a soft, warm breeze blowing in the office. It was the same breeze I had felt before at times when my father's energy came near. I began to feel the familiar sensation of floating an inch or two above my chair.

"What was your grandmother's name?" The words had come out of my mouth without my deciding to speak them.

"Margaret McCall," she answered.

Inside my head the conversation sped. "Oh, my God! Here I sit with a client who asked for a plain, old-fashioned psychotherapy session. I know, or at least I think I know, that somebody who is quite possibly her grandmother followed her in here for her session today. I'm quite comfortable with dead people floating around in my office, but what would she think of this? How on earth am I going to handle this one?"

I called on all the professionalism I could muster, and I succeeded in remaining moderately calm. I listened with one ear to my client and with the other ear to Margaret McCall. That session was a turning point in the client's therapy.

Months later I was able to tell my client about the experience, and her grandmother became a regular and very welcomed guest in our sessions.

***   ***   ***   ***   ***   ***   ***

One of my most useful miracles evolved out of my young son's habit of repeatedly losing his favorite friend—a ragged, dirty little bear. Bear used to go everywhere with Josh and was prone, as beloved and ragged bears usually are, to getting lost. Josh would plead with me many times every day to find his bear. One day he interrupted me from a meditation with his tale of woe. Bear was lost again. I noticed my right hand turning palm up for a few seconds. Then my hand turned over, palm down, and stretched out in front of me. My right hand had magically transformed into a Bear-finding sensor! Bear was hiding in a very obscure spot that day, but my right hand led me to him immediately. Josh was pleased but hardly impressed. The scene probably seemed quite normal from a four-year-old view of reality.

For many months I could use my right hand to find Bear and other lost objects around the house. Although my magic hand never seemed to me to contain the essence of my spiritual quest, it certainly was convenient.

*** *** *** *** *** *** ***

In his earthly life my Dad was a businessman. He always encouraged his children to study the basics of accounting and business, but all six of us rebelled against his advice. All six of us are now sorry.

The nursery demands serious business decisions from me almost daily. Most of them I make relatively comfortably. But one day in early February I was stumped. I had in front of me a proposal for a $6,000 automated irrigation system. I wondered: Should I buy the whole system? Should I buy part of it? And on what data could I base my decision?

The nursery was too young for me to be able to judge what our business volume might be for the coming spring, so I had no frame of reference for making such a major decision. In a state of mild despair, I retreated to the woods and sought privacy behind a greenhouse under tall pines. I calmed my mind and body, and I turned my thoughts upward. "Dad, please help. I do not know what to do."

I heard his answer clearly. He said, "Spend $4,000 on the irrigation system. Hold it to that figure for now. Your gross receipts for the spring season will be $32,000 and that will happen by May 10th."

I thanked Dad then went inside to write down his answers. I gave the go-ahead for $4,000 worth of pipes, risers, and sprinklers. Then I tucked the prediction concerning spring sales volume into a file and turned my attention to other matters.

At the end of May as I was doing all of the usual monthly bookkeeping tasks, I remembered the prediction. I retrieved it from the file and held it in my hand with a sense of increasing curiosity and excitement.

My system of bookkeeping did not allow me to analyze year-to-date figures on a daily basis, so I began punching numbers into my calculator to see how close Dad had been with his prediction. As the numbers printed out one by one, as the subtotals increased, and as the figures approached $30,000, my heart began to race. When the final total was clear, I sat in stunned silence.

A deposit was made on the morning of May 10. Gross year-to-date receipts after that deposit were $31,325.18. A deposit was made on the morning of May 11. Gross year-to-date receipts after that deposit were $33,090.31. Sometime during the day of May 10 receipts had crossed the $32,000.00 line.

I turned my face to the sky and, with tears streaming down my face, called out in excited appreciation, "Thank you, Dad! Thank you. But how did you know?"

I sensed Dad's loving smile and I heard the words, "You keep forgetting, baby—time is not linear."

***   ***   ***   ***   ***   ***   ***

A friend of mine introduced me to the book *The Findhorn Garden* (Harper & Row), a beautiful book describing the weaving together of the garden and Spirit. Given my intense interest in both, she and I shared a sense of surprise that I had not known of this book earlier.

As I began to read, I felt a wonderful sense of familiarity with the concepts and with the Findhorn approach to nurturing the earth and the plants that grow in it. Given my experiences with my father, it required only a slight readjustment in my thinking to imagine talking to broccoli spirits, petunia devas, and Landscape Angels. I was fascinated to read the advice the Findhorn gardeners received from the devas or guardian spirits of different plant species. Each deva spoke in a different style, emphasized different truths of the garden, and encouraged different techniques for the care of its species.

As I began to read the words of the daffodil deva, my body began to tingle with the electric sensation that inevitably means, "Open your ears and your eyes; something important is happening." As I read on I had the distinct impression that I had read these very words before. "But how could I have read these words before?" I thought. "I have had no awareness until now of devas or plant spirits. This must be a strange and inaccurate déjà vu."

I put the book down to follow the intensifying tingles to their answer. I remembered some words I had received in a meditation six months earlier. I went to my meditation notebook and searched until I found the right page. As always happens when a miracle materializes in front of my eyes, I was blissfully stunned.

These are the words of the daffodil deva in the *The Findhorn Garden*: "Everywhere we proclaim the triumphant message of rebirth, a new season. The air vibrates with this theme . . . Life is changing and always new. Just as you are different from what you were a year ago, so is each spring distinct, a newness to be specifically aware of. Respond, we say; all life is yours. Join us in the oneness of life and with us give eternal thanks to the One."

Six months earlier my hand had written: "Let me see through your eyes today this glory of the daffodils. Anew, anew. Renew. Spring is here. The goddess of the garden dwells in the spirit of eternal newness. Faith springing from the heights and the depths. Unending faith in newness. No, that is not the same daffodil as grew last spring. Nor are you the same person. The daffodil springs from the same bulb, but it is always anew. Glory to God!"

***   ***   ***   ***   ***   ***   ***

On a grey summer day, not unlike the day my father died, I felt drawn into a peaceful country church for my prayers and meditation. As I entered the empty sanctuary I heard a voice saying, "Do not go in today." The message made no sense to me, so I assumed that what I was hearing were the rumblings of my own mind.

I went into the church. I knelt at the altar for a few minutes and spoke to God. As I turned to walk to a pew, I heard a familiar voice saying, "Not today."

Stubbornly, I sat down. "Please come close, my friends," I pleaded, sending welcoming beams of love into the air around me. "Dad, where are you?" I heard no answers.

This was very odd. My friends in Spirit had been extremely reliable. They would speak with me about matters of great importance or trivia. They had always been willing to respond to me as long as I was in an open, receptive frame of mind. I checked my motivations—all clear and clean. I checked my behavior of the preceding days—no major mistakes or omissions to clean up before I could turn to Spirit. I checked my attitude—no interfering anger, bitterness, or malice. "What is the problem?" I implored.

I heard two messages and only two. They sounded as though were coming to me from a great distance. "First, this day, the. 13th, is not a good day. Second, be very cautious about asking for your own needs when someone else's needs are *truly* more important. Now, go about your day."

I was extremely confused. My Spirit friends had never slapped me on the hands like that before. I was painfully perplexed as to why my needs were important enough to warrant their time on other days but not on this day.

I went through the next few hours with feelings of confusion and loneliness lurking around me. Around 3:00 in the afternoon I felt a strong urge to call my sister-in-law, Carolyn, who was due to deliver a baby at any moment. I spoke to her. There were no signs of a baby being on its way.

Later in the afternoon a sudden and powerful wave of feeling swept over me. With no warning and for no discernible reason, I was overwhelmed by panic. I began anxiously pacing the living room floor, praying aloud. The words that spontaneously poured from my mouth surprised me. "Please, God, please go. Go now, *right now*. Be with that little girl. Let her be safe. Let her be born safely! God, I know I probably should be praying 'Thy will be done.' But if my wishes count for anything, listen to my will right now. Please, God, go!" An hour later my mother called to say that Carolyn was at the hospital in labor.

For the rest of the evening I felt a black cloud hanging over me. As I lay in bed that night, I had an odd fear that something was terribly wrong with my heart and that I might die in my sleep. I had learned by then that not all messages, whether they be from Spirit or from my own inner generator of mind garbage, are to be taken literally. Many messages are symbolic. With that reassurance, I was finally able to sleep.

During the night I dreamed there was a serious problem affecting my heart. I was very frightened and did not know where to turn for help. I remembered in the dream that a very dear college friend of mine had become a cardiologist. I was greatly relieved until I realized that if I called him he would not recognize my married name, and he might not help me. "I've got the solution," I thought excitedly in the dream. "I'll use my maiden name. I'll call Dave and say, 'This is Rebecca Stevens. This is *Rebecca Stevens*. Please help me!' " I felt confident I would be helped if I were Rebecca Stevens.

In the dream a doctor entered my hospital room. He was almost angelic in appearance and manner, and he brought good news. He said, "You are fine now. You are very lucky to be alive. A few more minutes of that and you couldn't have lived. The valve in your heart would have burst. You were in grave danger, but now you will be fine."

I awoke feeling tired and anxious. Moments later the phone rang. When I heard my brother's voice I asked, "Do we have a baby?" His answer was, "Yes, we have a little girl." I paused before asking the next question, feeling that I already knew its answer as well. "Did everything go OK?" Bill replied, "Everything is fine now, but there was trouble. During the labor, complications caused the baby to have a lot of stress on her heart. The doctors were so worried about her heart that they performed an emergency C-section. She and Carolyn are both fine now."

The tingles in my body were increasing. "And when was she born—the 13th?" "No," Bill answered, "she was born minutes after midnight. It was the 14th." "Thank God," I sighed, feeling a profound and mysterious sense of relief.

"And what is our little girl named?" Bill and Carolyn always selected names for their children before they were born, but they made a strict practice of telling no one. The child always heard its name first. Bill paused for a moment. Then he said gently, "She is named for you. She is Becca. She is Rebecca Stevens."

***   ***   ***   ***   ***   ***   ***

Someone much wiser than I must have determined that I was misusing my miracles, abusing the thrill of cavorting in the ethers. One day, all of a sudden and with no warning, the well went dry. No more miracles. I came crashing down into "reality" with such heaviness that it shook my faith in everything except despair. I went into spiritual DT's, craving "just one more little miracle—PLEASE!" I returned to the sites of previous miracles, listened to miracle music, and tried everything I could think of to eke just one teeny miracle out of the emptiness. A faint voice was audible in the cosmic distance. With great hope I called to it, "Voice, come closer, come closer with your little miracle!"

Voice: Sorry, ma'am. Plumb out of miracles.

Becca: How can you do this to me?

Voice: Do what?

Becca: Cut me off like this?

Voice: Cut you off from what?

Becca: Miracles, joker, miracles!

Voice: Oh, you thought those were miracles? Well, now, one or two of those happenings did approach miracle status. But all of those? No, no. Those weren't "real" miracles. They were just appetizers. You know—stuff to whet the appetite for the main course.

Becca (her passion cooling noticeably): Main course? Well, thanks, but I'm not really all that hungry. I'd settle for leftover appetizers if you have any extras.

Voice: Sorry, ma'am. Plumb out.

Becca: OK, OK. What's on the menu for the main course?

Voice: Sign here. Dotted line.

Becca: I asked what's on the menu, not for the contract.

Voice: Sorry, ma'am. That's not how we do things around here.

Becca: Could you tell me what I'm signing up for?

Voice: Life.

Becca: Do any details come with this marvelous offer?

Voice: Details? Sure, details. Let's see—here it is. It says "LIFE: With all that it can offer as a course in soul development." How's that?

Becca: Vague. Let me ask it this way. What are my options?

Voice: Option One, sign here. Option Two, don't.

Becca: And a few details, please, on Option Two.

Voice: You already know all about Option Two. Pretend to live, assume you already know what you need to know, turn a deaf ear to your soul, and rob yourself of life at every chance you get. Option Two, part two, goes like this: By not actively and passionately turning toward your soul, you turn away. Bye bye, soul. Bye bye, God. Bye bye, light. Hello, dark. Get the picture?

Becca: Pen, please. Hello, dotted line. By the way, who are you?

Voice: One small voice in the choir of your soul.

CHAPTER THREE:

THE FIRST LESSON

During the early months of my journey I believed that it was my father who had made all of the arrangements for my miracles. I thought it was always my father's voice that I heard during my heavenly hallucinations and it was always my father's hand that wrote through mine. His energy felt clear and always present. I innocently assumed he was my one and only cosmic buddy.

Slowly, even reluctantly, I began to sense the presence of other souls around me. Initially I resisted their intrusion into what felt like a very private relationship between my father and me. Their persistence was gentle and steady, and gradually I began to relax my grip on my father's arm.

During a meditation one day I felt a new and yet oddly familiar energy in the air. It was a different vibration, as metaphysical folks would say. It is not easy to describe in words how the energy was different. It is no simple task for an earthbound being to describe the precise ways in which one dead person floating in the air feels different from another. However, the new energy seemed to be male, older than my father, and wiser than my father. He seemed strong and yet extremely gentle and patient. He felt to me like a very old friend. My trust in this new soul quickly grew, and soon I relaxed and gave in to him.

"My name is O-S-I-R-I-N," he wrote through my pen. "I have been with you forever. Welcome back to our home. Welcome, little one."

Our re-introduction was simple, yet his energy totally capti-
vated me. I thought of him as often as a teenager thinks of her
newest love. In the days that followed I beckoned to him often,
asking him to come close, to teach me, to accept me as his
friend and student. I did not yet know who he was except that
his name was Osirin and that he was filled with wisdom. It
seemed he held the answers to questions I was not yet wise
enough to ask.

Osirin's presence soon became a profound and compelling
influence in my mind. I turned to him many times every day,
asking him to open my ears to his wisdom. Sometimes he
spoke softly in my mind; at other times he took my pen and
wrote. His words began to flow in sweet sounds and rhythms,
in lovely images. Osirin wrote in poems, in metaphors, in tales
and yarns. His words touched my heart in a way that brought
me a profound sense of peace and love.

"Osirin, who are you?" I asked.

"You'll know soon enough, little one. For today, let us speak
of stardust."

And so we did. He began by saying, "We will call this lesson
STARDUST. Now listen, little one. Relax your hand and your
ears. Don't think. Just listen and write. Let me have the pen.
Better. Relax more. Go away, mind, go. Come closer, heart.
Thank you. That's better.

"Little bits of stardust fall from the heavens every moment.
Each bit of stardust holds a truth. Perhaps that truth is but a
tiny one, a mere grain of sand on the beach. Do not minimize
one truth. Do not minimize one slight glimpse of your soul.
Deep within the one is the All.

"Sometimes you act as though what you seek is outside yourself. Sometimes you seem to believe that your miracles exist in
something that you think of as an outer world. Yet, what you
seek is you. It is within you; it is through you. What you seek
is your soul."

We had only begun our lesson, just rekindled our friendship,
yet I strongly felt that I knew this soul. I was surprised at the
love that flowed between us. I was surprised at the comfort and
trust I felt with him.

"Osirin, I don't know my soul," I said. "I believe that I have a soul, but I do not know who or what she is. If I have a soul, why doesn't she come to me like you do? Why won't my soul talk to me? Osirin, I don't understand."

Osirin answered, "Your soul has more sense than to appear to you today in all of her power. She would hardly want to blow all your physical fuses with a premature grand appearance! Strengthen your belief in your soul and in her connection with God. Ready yourself. Seek her. Ask for her. Follow her. Listen for her soft voice. Trust her. Let her take your hand and your heart. Be her."

"What do I do? How do I proceed?"

"Be a hunter of stardust," he said. "Gather it fresh. Protect and preserve it."

"How?" I asked with growing frustration.

"Did not Jesus say, 'Seek and ye shall find'? I will show you bits of stardust, but you must be the gatherer. You must be hungry for truth. Go now. There's a bit of stardust floating in the air over there. Make it your own."

***　　***　　***　　***　　***　　***　　***

It was not at all clear to me how one goes about gathering stardust. Osirin wrote to me of trust, beauty, and love, but he would not tell me how to gather stardust. After many futile attempts, pleading with him to spoonfeed truth to me in a palatable and easily digestible form, I realized that I would have to struggle to gather stardust myself. So I began looking around me. I began to look for meaning in everything I encountered. Every time I saw a movie I would consciously ask Osirin to point out the one scene or the one line that held a lesson for me. I did the same with books I read. I frequented book stores, asking Osirin to pull me toward books that would be good teachers for me. I scanned books that held no conscious interest for me, letting myself ask why I had been drawn to them.

I listened to music at every chance I got. I had tapes for the car, tapes for walking, tapes for meditating, and tapes for the tub. I developed a great fondness for modern black gospel music and found it very uplifting. It is often filled with the joy and fun of faith—feelings that were all too rare in my religious upbringing. I listened to love songs, seeing within each one (at least each good one) a message of love that transcends human relationships. I imagined each love song being sung by me to Spirit. I would listen again, imagining the same song being sung by Spirit to me. Songs that were special I listened to hundreds of times.

I spent more quiet time in my garden. I shoveled and weeded less; I sat more. I indulged less in my favorite hobby of constantly redesigning the garden. Instead, I watched the plants grow, I talked to them, and I asked them to teach me the secrets they knew. I imagined meaning in each flower, in each stone, and in the patterns of tree branches as they reached to the sky.

I listened carefully to the conversations I had with my son, Josh. I listened for the wisdom that came effortlessly from his mouth. I listened as he explained the meaning of life and love, delighting in the truths that his four-year-old mind could comprehend with ease.

I asked Osirin for assistance during therapy sessions, trusting that with his help I would hear more and learn more from my clients. I trusted my clients to ask me the questions to which I most needed answers. I trusted my mouth to answer their questions, and I trusted my ears to listen carefully to the answers that came.

I reminded myself dozens of times each day to look around for stardust. "Wake up, self. Look with new eyes. What is in front of you right now is one peony blossom. Don't look at that peony as part of the garden design. Look into that peony. It is just as likely that truth lives inside of that peony as anywhere else. Slow down, self, slow down."

Very gradually my eyes began to perceive bits and pieces of truth. There was no coherent whole, no unified Meaning of Life. What I collected were morsels of meaning, tasty tidbits of truth, nuggets of wisdom. All the pieces in my growing collection of truths reinforced my belief. The belief grew stronger. It inspired most of my waking hours. I began to feel lonely when I lost it and confused when I forgot it. The belief gradually

became the cornerstone of my life. I believed:
There is Something Out There Worth Knowing!

***   ***   ***   ***   ***   ***   ***

"Osirin, Osirin. Who are you?"

"My name is Osirin. I am the one who has written to you
often before. My words flow like dew drops from a flower . . .
softly. My light shines to you from the rays of God's light. It
penetrates you with the power of a laser and with the softness
of a gentle kiss upon your brow. I am your guru. I give you
love, wisdom, guidance. I have great power upon which you
can call at any time.

"I am the one who has led you safely out of the jaws of lions.
Your life has been directed toward this place because I was
leading you here. Your light almost went out eight years ago,
but you listened to me, little one. You listened and you were
led. Your light was rekindled.

"You have seen me before and you will see me again. I met
your father on the other side and was with him when he appeared to you. Oh, little one, how wide were your eyes on that
day! Lucky father, lucky daughter."

***   ***   ***   ***   ***   ***   ***

During the stardust days I frequented empty churches as
often as I could. I found a favorite church on each side of town
so I could stop at whichever sanctuary I was near. Most
churches exude positive energy from their walls and their
pews. The formality and boredom that often fill them on Sunday morning evaporates by Sunday afternoon and only the
love and sincerity of true seekers is left behind. That is the
energy I selfishly soaked up during the weekdays when nobody else was around.

As I entered the doors of my favorite country church, I
sensed a strong energy in the air. I knelt at the altar, offering
my thanks to God for the beauty and bounty of my journey. I
left Him two daffodils in the baptismal font and sat down in a
pew.

Becca: Osirin, your presence feels very strong today.

Osirin: Yes, little one. We begin a new lesson today.

Becca: I am ready.

Osirin: It is time to learn trust.

Becca (breathing a long and relaxed sigh): Ahhh, an easy lesson. I am glad to learn whatever you have to teach me about trust, although I think this will be like teaching a child to like candy. Trust has always been natural and easy for me, Osirin. You know that. But I welcome your teachings.

Osirin: Then we begin at the beginning. After all, without trust this journey will be treacherous and fraught with danger. With trust, this journey will be merely terrifying.

Becca (with self-assurance noticeably lessened): But I know about trust, Osirin. I do well at trust.

Osirin: So it would seem.

Becca: I know that tone in your voice. I think I am in for a surprise. OK, friend, let me hear it.

Osirin: What you have called trust has little to do with what you must learn. Expecting a fellow human to do what he says he will do is not trust. That is merely your desire for certainty. Expecting other people to treat you kindly is not trust. That is merely your desire for comfort. Often when you say to a person, "I trust you," you simply mean, "I have concluded that you are a sufficiently rigid being that you will not change in ways that will surprise me and necessitate my being real with both of us." That kind of "trust" does you no good on this journey.

Becca: Help me, Osirin. I'm confused and scared. I feel ignorant; no, I feel *stupid*. Take my hand. I'll go with you, but I am scared.

***   ***   ***   ***   ***   ***   ***

Osirin took my hand just as I asked. The touch of his hand against mine was so light, however, that only in moments of deep trust could I feel him by my side. Trust and trust alone was my ticket of passage to the feeling I desired—profound closeness to my beloved guru. It was only unquestioning trust in Osirin that seemed powerful enough to open my ears to his words and my heart to his presence. And only within the deepest state of trust could I experience the most priceless gift of all—a glimpse, a taste, a hint of the Peace that passeth all understanding.

The gift of peace was an elusive one. Sometimes meditation would bring a bit of it to my heart, sometimes not. Sometimes trips to church altars or quiet moments in my garden would remind me of its sweetness, sometimes not.

The sweet, brief tastes of the peace and wisdom that Osirin possessed converted me into a junkie, and I longed for more. My longing turned to craving, and with craving came both frustration and urgency. I have made many mistakes along my path, but the first costly one was elevating my newly acquired addiction to peace onto the pedestal of the sublime.

I could not yet see that addiction and peace are mutually exclusive states of being, even if the addiction is to a lofty and spiritual goal. I did not yet understand that attempts to wrench peace from Osirin accomplished nothing other than hurtling me off my path. In my ignorance, fueled by the fire of craving, I began demanding that Osirin make himself and his peace easier for me to find, and that he do so on my terms.

"Osirin," I demanded of him, "it's been days since I've heard you clearly and felt you nearby. You've done nothing lately to show me that you are here. Please, do something! If you don't see fit to materialize as Dad did, then some concrete little miracle would suffice. I want to feel more peace. I want to understand it better, and I know I can't do that without your help. Why won't you help me?"

"Trust me, little one," he replied with his characteristic softness.

"I do trust you, Osirin. But you're not doing anything these days. Give me something to trust you for. *Do something!*"

***   ***   ***   ***   ***   ***   ***

Soon thereafter it felt to me as though Osirin disappeared. I could no longer hear him speak. I couldn't feel his energy. When I meditated I felt like an engine idling at 3,000 r.p.m.— still on the outside but racing on the inside. I could not quiet my thoughts. I could not find meaning anywhere. I was tired, bored, irritable, and empty.

For almost two weeks I felt very discouraged. I made many

half-hearted attempts to meditate. I prayed many prayers that were very nearly sincere. When nothing worked, I became enraged at Osirin.

"How dare you!" I raged at him. "You lead me this far, you get me hooked, and then you back out. What kind of trick is this? What kind of loving energy is this that you deliver in a package of abandonment? I have had it. You come to me this time. You seek me out. You owe me an apology!"

Osirin did not answer me. As I was later to learn, rage and despair never coax Osirin to be near. But they make a delectable bait that Voice of Doubt cannot resist.

"Do you finally see?" asked Voice of Doubt. "I warned you about over-romanticizing this stuff. Looks like the honeymoon is over."

"Maybe so," I replied. "But maybe it's me. Maybe I'm doing something wrong."

"If he really loved you, he would show you if you were doing something wrong, wouldn't he?"

"I guess so. I don't know."

"And look at what has happened lately," Voice of Doubt said smugly. "Look at your hit rate."

I knew what Voice of Doubt was speaking of. In the past two weeks I had failed at meditation and at prayer. I had failed at hearing Osirin's words in my mind or through my pen. In addition to those failures, I had made ten psychic predictions and they had all been wrong. All ten were simple yes/no guesses, and all of them had been wrong.

"I know, I know," I conceded. "I've been off for a while."

"Off hardly describes it. You have bombed out. And your illusory cosmic friends have abandoned you."

"This is hard enough without your negativity. Go away."

"I do not abandon you."

"I should only be so lucky as to have you abandon me, V.D."

"Look at the evidence," Voice of Doubt chided. "Look at how often they have failed you. And look at how often you have failed. Ten times."

Voice of Doubt very nearly persuaded me. If it had not been for those tingles that began to excite my cells, I probably would have thrown in the towel and admitted spiritual defeat.

But the tingles began to arouse my sleeping awareness. Suddenly it was clear.

"Wait!" I exclaimed. "Do you realize what that means? My God! Those were all yes/no predictions and I was wrong every time. The statistical odds of that—let's see—what is the formula? Point five to the tenth power. This is incredible! There is less than one chance in a thousand that I could have been that dumb without their help. They were here all along. They have been trying to get through to me and this is the only way they could. They didn't leave me, V.D. *I left them.* I've been stubborn, selfish, and demanding. I've closed my eyes, stuffed cotton in my ears, and worn armor over my heart. I left them. Osirin, I'm here. I'm here and I'm sorry. So very sorry."

      ***   ***   ***   ***   ***   ***   ***

The next day as I sat in a church garden Osirin spoke. "Hello, little one of the garden. I brought to you a new friend. Her name is Ophelia. Welcome her."

"Where have you been?" asked Ophelia. "Lights glow and all is well. Now, about being left alone. Abandonment is an illusion. What you call abandonment is merely the voice in the darkness—your own voice in your own darkness. Abandonment is not possible in Spirit, simply not possible. Think—who abandons whom? You feel left alone. Be alone, but not a-lone. Be with all and alone. No one is more alone than another. No one is un-alone or unlone. No one is together with any energy but his own—ever. See your loneliness. See your true lone-lee-ness, lone-lea-ness."

I was so glad to have Osirin by my side again that I overlooked the cryptic nature of Ophelia's words. I didn't know who this disembodied lady was, but if she was a friend of Osirin's, she was okay with me. For the moment I simply relaxed and floated in the lovely energy of my reunion with my friends.

When I transcribed my scribbled notes later that evening, I was confused about what Ophelia was trying to teach me. I pondered her words slowly and carefully. "See your true lone-lee-ness, lone-lea-ness," she had said. I felt compelled to look

up the words lee and lea in my dictionary. I was amazed as I
read their meanings. Lee is the safe side or haven, and lea is a
garden. Her lesson was clear:

Loneliness means to be in the safe garden of the self.

***　　***　　***　　***　　***　　***　　***

Ophelia's teachings had been timely and deeply healing. I
felt fond of her immediately, but I still ached for Osirin. I had
missed him. My anger and stubbornness had kept me distant
from him for weeks, and I longed to have him near again. His
words always touched me in a way no one's ever had, and his
presence always brought me peace. Being cautious to sound
very undemanding, I humbly invited him to come close. And I
waited.

Osirin's energy always approaches very softly. I often do not
know he has arrived until I hear his voice gently echoing in
the front of my forehead, half inside and half outside my skull.
I sat quietly, waiting, asking him to come. I heard his voice
saying, "A pen, please, little one," and I began to write his
words.

"Trust in me, little one. My love for you is not of the earth.
My love for you is made of the stuff of God's light. My love
cannot disappear or fade. My wisdom cannot decay. My soul
cannot dim. Stay near and strengthen your trust. Faith is not
something that you feel. It is something that you do. Be faith.
Through faith and trust you will begin to learn love—real love,
the love of which we speak and the love I give to you.

"Doubt us no more, little one. Your home, your haven of
safety and light, has always been with us. Nothing has
changed. You have only come home . . . home. We are welcoming you with all our hearts. Release your doubt, and open your
heart to us in total trust. No doubt means no pain. Welcome
home."

***　　***　　***　　***　　***　　***　　***

Practicing trust became my favorite pastime. I was so deeply
grateful for Osirin's reassurances and for my lesson in trust
that I longed to reinforce my learning in any way I could.

Every little trauma I encountered offered me a chance to practice. Every flaring of my temper offered me the opportunity to turn to Osirin in trust. Every moment of doubt or despair presented one more mini-lesson. I grew more and more comfortable with trust and became a junior pro at turning away from doubt. I knelt often before God, thanking Him for the ambassador who had taught me this lesson and relinquishing more and more of my willfulness to Him. I felt deeply grateful, and I let my gratitude be known.

I had mastered one lesson. I had learned that the love of Spirit is absolutely reliable. I knew that whatever doubts I harbored in my mind were my own "fault." I felt a great liberation in understanding that my pain was of my own creating and my beloved Spirits grieved when I chose to torture myself. The idea that God or loving souls in Spirit could abandon me was erased from my mind. I was lighter, freer, and happier. I breathed a deep sigh of relief.

As I breathed that sigh of relief, I noticed a new lesson approaching from a distance. "Oh, no. No, please. Wait at least another week. No more lessons yet. No, no, no!"

Sighs of relief are invitations to lessons that are sitting on the horizon, waiting to pounce on the next ready student. I had already sighed. No amount of quick and deep inhaling could take back that sigh, although I tried. Even before I recovered from hyperventilation I found myself in the midst of round two of the lesson on abandonment and trust.

*** *** *** *** *** *** ***

It was one of those months. Everywhere I turned, earthlings were doing everything they could to mess up my life. All of my psychotherapy clients had crises at the same time, and most of them expected me to fix their crises pronto. My previously delightful and nearly enlightened four-year-old decided to enter a horrendous developmental stage, and he became a monster overnight. My family life seemed the epitome of uncertainty and instability. Chaos broke out at the nursery, and trouble was being generated by employees, customers, suppliers, and everybody else who could find a way to wreak havoc in my life.

I averted a few catastrophes, doctored other people's battered feelings, bailed myself and a few friends out of assorted dilemmas, patched a few sinking ships, warred against several bad guys, and practiced trust through it all. Then I collapsed.

As I fell to the ground in exhaustion I managed to produce one last burst of energy, just enough energy to scream at Osirin.

Becca: This is ridiculous! And on top of ridiculous, it's unfair. Grossly unfair. I spend my time practicing trust and other folks spend their time practicing ways to screw up my life. There's no one down here to count on. Everybody is pulling dirty punches, and you expect me to be trusting? Where is the fairness in that? Where is the common sense in that?

Osirin: Hello, busy one. You have been so busy with your projects that you have forgotten me.

Becca: Forgotten you? Osirin, I've been out on the front lines getting shot at lately. I've screamed and yelled for you. I've implored you! How on earth—I mean, oh, you know what I mean—how on *anywhere* can you be telling me that I forgot about you?

Osirin: The war you have pretended to be fighting is not the real war. It is a distraction. You take it so seriously that your mind is filled with its sounds and its noises. My voice is soft, little one. My voice cannot override the volume of your distractions. I did come to you, but you did not hear me.

Becca (her fires beginning to cool): But, Osirin, my family, my business, my clients, my son—they are not the real war?

Osirin: No, little one. Soft now. Quiet.

Becca: Help me, Osirin. Help me.

Osirin: Let your tears cleanse your mind. No more anger. No more rage against those people who have not abandoned you at all. Come closer and look. See the white light streaming toward you, showering all around you.

Little one, as you struggle with the wars of your earthly existence, remember me. Do not call to me only in your moments of quiet. Call to me, little one, in your moments of struggle as well.

You have been too busy for me, too enmeshed in your attempts to solve your problems and conquer your dilemmas.

Sometimes solving your problems solves little, and conquering your dilemmas may win you no medals. The peace of the heart is won only through love, little one. Only through love.

You turn to other humans expecting them to fill your heart with peace. Listen slowly, little one, very slowly. Peace lives within you. No human can give it to you, for peace is a gift only God is entitled to give. Let me teach you inner peace so that you may share it with others, but do not look to them to give it to you. And, little one, do not rage against them when you lose it.

Human love can fill you with the pleasures of earth. It can lift you toward the stars. It can bring light to your eyes and a smile to your lips. It can fill your heart with a sweet remembrance of that which is Divine. But, my dear little one, no human can bring the light to your soul. No human ever has. Please hear now. No human ever has. No human has ever given you the light, no human can ever take it away, and no human can return it to you if you have set it down along the path.

Your wars in these weeks have been struggles of the earth plane. They are not wrong or bad, but they are not of Light. Success in those wars will never rekindle a dimmed light.

So, now rest. Peace to you, deep into your heart. Rest. Rest now from the wars whose victories bring only pain.

CHAPTER FOUR:

RETURNING THE KEYS

My communication with Osirin was renewed and refreshed. I heard his words clearly once again. Except for the fatigue I often felt in my writing arm, receiving wisdom from him was almost effortless. I became confident, relaxed, and comfortable. Gradually I began to feel I had an "in" in the big skies. At some point I must have crossed the fine line that lies between confident and cocky. Osirin didn't like it, and he tested me once again.

"I have an important lesson for you today, little one. Are you ready?" Osirin asked.

"Oh, of course, Osirin. I'm ready for anything!" I was brimming over with kindergartener confidence. I had learned that 1+1=2 and even that 10+10=20. I arrogantly assumed I was ready for advanced spiritual calculus.

"Then listen carefully, little one. This is your lesson: The principals are principled, and the principles are non-entities."

"And what else?" I asked.

"Nothing else," was Osirin's terse reply.

"What on earth does that mean?"

Osirin was silent.

"Tell me, please. What does it mean?"

"Ah," said Osirin, "behold a confused girl."

***   ***   ***   ***   ***   ***   ***

Osirin wrote no more and left me to my own devices. At first I mocked this lesson, thinking that he merely taunted me with philosophical nonsense. I was defiant for a day or so, refusing to indulge in his silly game. He stayed patiently, but quietly, by my side as a loving parent would do with a child throwing a tantrum. He refused to speak, he refused to write, and he produced absolutely no miracles, small or large.

A few days later I found myself walking into a book store with no idea why I was doing so. For reasons I did not yet understand, I walked toward the dictionaries and began flipping through them. "This is an odd thing for me to do in a bookstore," I thought. My fingers turned to the p's, and I began looking up the words "principle" and "principal." I hurriedly pulled out a piece of paper and wrote what I found. Obscure definitions jumped out at me. I wrote down everything I could find in every dictionary on the shelves, then I left the store with the vague sense that Noah Webster and I had just had a very important rendezvous.

Once at home I found a large piece of construction paper and made a huge map. At the top of the page I wrote the sentence, "The principals are principled, and the principles are nonentities." Underneath each word I wrote all the definitions I had been able to find. I omitted "the" and "are," assuming that I knew their meanings. Osirin smiled his cosmic smile over my shoulder as I pieced together my definitions.

When my map was complete, I could sense lines across the page. The lines led me to the meaning of Osirin's teaching.

"Osirin, it makes sense! It really does!" The lines traversing the page led me to the understanding that Spirit holds the keys, yet the keys themselves do not exist. Only with the aid of Spirit will the key open The Door.

I could see the mistake I had been making. I had become enamored of keys and had tried to collect them. I collected miracles as though they were tickets to paradise; I collected Osirin's words as though they were proof of my spiritual OK-ness; I collected my growing psychic powers as though they were jewels in my celestial crown. Until that moment I had not understood that without the love and wisdom of Spirit, the keys I thought I held would repeatedly dissolve in my still-human hands.

"Osirin, this is amazing!" I searched my mind for every key I could find and gladly returned each one to my beloved friend.

Osirin took the keys, and as he left he gently said, "Just remember, little one, that without God, truth is irrelevant."

CHAPTER FIVE:

THE LESSON ON FEAR

As I review the early years of my journey, all the lessons taught to me by Spirit seem clear and distinct. As they were taught, however, they were intertwined, one lesson often being enmeshed with another. Lessons on trust were spiced with a few tasty morsels on love. Lessons on abandonment were lightened by messages on joy. And, since time is not linear to folks without bodies, my teachers did not feel compelled to present lessons in any sort of linear order. I was often tested on the material in Chapter Ten before I had even been shown Chapter Two.

Lessons appeared when I least expected them and sometimes when I least wanted them. Lessons usually made very little sense to me at first, their wisdom unfolding only as I struggled to master the mysteries that I found perched on the end of my nose. I rarely welcomed lessons as they began, for lesson time always meant work—very hard work.

If I had known what was in store for me, I would most certainly have fled from the lesson on fear. I never would have claimed mastery over fear, as I had naively claimed mastery in the area of trust. I knew I was afraid of fear—no doubt about it! So Osirin eased me into the lesson.

I had some friends and colleagues who were researching a case in which a teenage girl was experiencing recurrent spontaneous psychokinesis (RSPK). Her story hit the newspaper presses around the world as objects in her home began to fly through the air.

My friends asked me if I would be interested and willing to spend some time with Sandra when she was brought to our area for testing and evaluation. I told my friends I would consider it. I talked at length with Osirin, Dad, and Ophelia. All of my heavenly friends encouraged me to get involved, telling me they would accompany me in this experience. So I agreed.

Judging from other poltergeist cases, history suggested that when the person who possessed RSPK was in an environment other than the "hot" one, objects obeyed the laws of physics and gravity and did not pretend to be airplanes. That is what we expected to happen with Sandra, and that is what did happen during the first five days of her visit. There were no flying objects. None.

On the sixth day I was spending a few hours with Sandra. By that time she and I had developed a rather close relationship. We were in my office at the nursery, talking about nothing in particular. Sandra came over to me to give me a hug. As we hugged, I noticed a pencil fall to the floor. I thought it was curious, but I paid little attention. After all, pencils have been known to fall to the floor before. It was hardly a startling experience.

A bottle cap lay on the bookshelf beside the pencil that had fallen. Sandra's arms were still around me and her back was to the bookshelf. I noticed the bottle cap sailing through the air and landing across the room. My mind began to race. Could it be happening? Surely not.

It *was* happening, and the energy intensified very quickly. I took Sandra by the hand to lead her out of my office. As we neared the office door the telephone flew off my desk, sailed through the air, and struck Sandra forcefully in the back. I knelt on the floor beside Sandra to comfort her in her physical pain and emotional despair.

My mind was split in half. Half of me was talking to Sandra and making decisions about what to do next. The other half of me was calling desperately to Osirin for help.

Never before had I been in the presence of an energy that felt so unknown, so unpredictable and so unfriendly. There were no laws of physics to explain what was happening. Reality as I knew it had suddenly become irrelevant. Even the most fundamental laws and assumptions I had believed in, even that of gravity, were instantaneously shattered. I felt like I was in a void—in a terrifying place where nothing made sense. Perhaps it was a benign void, perhaps a treacherous one. I did not know. Nothing made sense and there was absolutely nobody who could give me an understanding of this energy. There was nobody who could protect me.

I had neither the time nor the energy in that moment to feel angry or abandoned. I was poignantly aware of my aloneness, my complete aloneness. But that mattered little. I found myself facing a much more serious dilemma than abandonment or loneliness. I was face to face with the void. And I was terrified.

Things kept flying. Doors opened and closed unaided. One door slammed viciously into Sandra's face. As I drove with Sandra away from the nursery, my car repeatedly slipped out of gear. Telephone lines disconnected or screeched with a piercing shrillness as I tried to make calls in her presence. Lamps fell over. Even a tube of Crest toothpaste got into the act, fulfilling its inner wish to fly.

There was a greyness around me. My skin felt clammy, my stomach slightly nauseous. I felt a thick, heavy energy in the air. I did what I could to calm Sandra, and I coped with this bizarre twist of un-reality by doing the practical things that had to be done.

I returned Sandra to the colleague of mine with whom she was staying, explained the events of the afternoon, and left for home. As I drove home alone, my car kindly helped to ease my anxiety by changing gear only when I gave the manual command. When I entered my home, I feared that the air would still be sticky with eery, grey energy. But it wasn't. Telephones resumed their normal behavior, doors opened and closed only at the touch of a human hand, and objects around the house obeyed the laws of conventional earth-physics.

I tried to relax, but my body would not comply. Inside of me I still stood facing the void. It felt to me like a dark chasm. It felt like hell. I didn't know then and I don't know now why flying telephones and soaring toothpaste tubes would bring me to the edge of hell, but they did. To this day I do not know whether flying telephones are good, bad, or neutral, but one of them escorted me to the void which I needed to explore.

I doubt that I would have ever chosen to peer into the void had I felt any choice. I doubt that I would have ever elected to look deep into the pit of my inner fears and panic. But I had no choice. That was clear. No matter what I saw, I could not endure the tension and anxiety any longer. So I looked. In the void, shining and loving, was God.

My vision of God occurred so quickly that I have no memory of how He looked. But I will never forget the feeling. White light surrounded me, and I knew I was safe. It became totally irrelevant whether the energy that makes telephones fly is good or bad. The power source that energized the flying phone could have been powerfully misdirected adolescent anger; it could have been a logically explainable irregularity in electromagnetic energy fields; it could have been feisty or playful spirits; or it could have been the disembodied soul of the Marquis de Sade. It did not matter. All that mattered was God and the energy that surrounded me. I fell exhausted into His arms, my energy so totally spent that fear dissolved into sweet and peaceful calm.

*** *** *** *** *** *** ***

In the weeks that followed I re-experienced fear in many situations. I imagine that the intensity of views into one's panic pit rarely subsides overnight. The reverberations from my experience were noisy and uncomfortable.

I asked questions of the few people I knew who just might have the answer. "What makes telephones fly?" I asked. The ideas they presented to me didn't help. I turned to Osirin with the same question, "What makes telephones fly?" Osirin gave me several poetic analogies and images, but even his explanations did not help to reduce my nagging anxiety.

It slowly became clear to me that I didn't care why telephones fly. This was not a lesson given to me to teach the principles of altered or alternative energy patterns in the universe. This lesson was not about poltergeists or cosmic troublemakers. This lesson was not about psychic voodoo or telephone levitation. This lesson was not about what happens when Ma

Bell takes to the skies. This lesson was about fear. Once I understood that, I began to ask the right questions and to listen for answers that held the wisdom I needed.

I spent a lot of time with Osirin during those weeks. Fear crept into my mind often, and Osirin gently and persistently taught me. "These are days of trials," he said. "The problem lies in not clearly seeing the truth. Your old views invade. Fear creeps and crawls. What I want you to do is this: Try to ignore the doubts and the fears. Remember that you know nothing. What you feel is irrelevant to what is true. Never confuse the two right now. Never confuse what you feel with what is true. You must remember that you know nothing. Nothing. Peace comes in the void. Peace comes only in the void. Be slow. You know nothing, so conclude nothing. Renew your belief in us."

Later he said, "There is time, little one. There is time for you to see. Open your eyes very slowly so that you won't be scared. I am here, nearby. Little one, you are so tired. We're helping."

Osirin's next comfort to me was, "Do not stop mid-stream. You are protected. Go forth with faith in me. Your faith will renew you and speed you on. I ask only what you are capable of giving. Fear me not. Fear yourself not. Struggle for me. Let this be your lesson: Faith is a journey of heart, mind, and will. Waver not. I will lead you if you will only believe. Follow my light."

Later he said, "Let no obstacle appear real or barrier feel to be of stone. Go forward. No fear, little one. No fear.

"Be free, little one, be free! No power is too great for you to handle. You are a person. You are not a god, not a slave— neither an eagle nor a worm. Be all of you with no fear. Let your light be at times a candle flicker and at times the power of the lightning. Leave your pain, leave your powerlessness. And, once and for all, leave your fear."

*** *** *** *** *** *** ***

Little by little Osirin's words began to penetrate the inner-most parts of my heart. Finally one day I could see.

"I think I've got it, Osirin. I think I've finally got it. For the first time in my life I've looked fear in the eye instead of running from it. I can see now that with you by my side and with God's love as my armor, there is nothing to fear. Fear is the crippler, not flying phones or topsy-turvy reality or even the pit itself. Fear is the enemy. Whenever I give in to fear, I turn my back on you. Osirin, facing fear is so hard, so very hard. I'm exhausted, but finally I see. As long as I stay close to you, there is nothing to fear. Absolutely *nothing* to fear."

"It's time now to rest, little one," Osirin gently replied. "Rest. Rest for many days, and rest in my love. Little one, the lights shine brightly but not constantly. Recognize the gentler lights, those that shine in dew drops and in children's tears. Recognize Spirit in each blossom. Surround yourself with softness. Be gentle with yourself. Your journey has been fast and hectic. You are not lost, only at a docking station. We are moors, harbors, pilots, and lighthouses. Fear not, as you will now begin to rest. Rest is essential on our side, too. Remember cycles of growth; remember that nothing can grow at all times. Remember that and despair not. Be in harbor. Enjoy it. Much will be asked of you later, so peace now, little one. I am close but quiet. Ask me not to write for a week or so. I am composing volumes for later. But rest for me, too, little one. My love."

***　　***　　***　　***　　***　　***　　***

Many months later—

Becca: Osirin, that was quite a lesson, the flying phones and all. Was that the advanced course in fear and trust?

Osirin: An advanced course. Not necessarily *the* advanced course.

Becca: Osirin, in the days when I was deciding whether to spend time with Sandra, you strongly encouraged me to proceed. It sounded as though everything would be fine. Did I hear you wrong? Did I make up those conversations in my head? Did I hear what I wanted to hear? Did you lie to me?

Osirin: Little one, slow. If I had told you what was entailed, would you have signed up?

Becca: Touché.

CHAPTER SIX:

LETTING GO

Gradually the lessons on fear receded in their prominence and intensity. I was relieved. By that time I knew the journey would not be easy—at least not for a long while. On the easy days I delighted in the little miracles that had returned to my life. I was careful to breathe no sighs of relief, careful to acknowledge the next lesson that was sitting on the horizon, and careful to admit my total lack of power over the lesson's choice as to when it wished to appear. Lessons, it seems, can be appeased by the student's humility. They can be coaxed into delaying their arrival by awareness on the student's part of her total ignorance and stupidity. Cockiness, on the other hand, is a temptation that no self-respecting lesson can resist.

*** *** *** *** *** *** ***

As I meditated one day I felt a very playful energy approaching. "Who is this cosmic comic?" I wondered. As he came closer and took my hand, I felt Osirin's wonderfully familiar energy.

Becca: What is it, my playful friend? What is so funny today?

Osirin: Smile, little one. Shall we play a game?

Becca: Yes! That's a great idea.

Osirin: Then I shall write you a missive. Look up these words—look up missive and missile.

Becca: OK. Missive means a written communication, a letter intended to be sent. Missile means an object thrown or projected.

Osirin: So, what shall we write today? Do you wish us to write a missive or a missile or a mission. Look that up, too, while you're at it. And go to definition number 4.

Becca: Mission, definition number 4, is a specific task with which a person or a group is charged.

Osirin: So, of what shall we write? The missive? The mission?

Becca: Anything, my friend. You choose.

Osirin: Then I will write of love, because of that there is plenty. And of other things there is less. Missions come and go. Love does not. Missives are mailed and they are read and they end. Love does not end. Let's have some poetry. What do you say?

Becca: I say fine!

Osirin: Shall we poetize a rose? No, too many meanings. Shall we perchance chance a daffodil? No, too wintry outside. Well, let it be the color gold. Gold is yellow highlighted. It is yellow mixed with God's white light. It is the earth that has sat on itself long enough to create a denseness of rare purity and virtue. Look up concourse.

Becca: Concourse is an act or process of coming together or merging; a meeting produced by spontaneous or voluntary coming together; an open space where roads or paths meet. Wow, that one has lots of poignant meanings!

Osirin: Course, of course, means path. Concourse always means with path. Why are you looking it up?

Becca: Because I just love it when you are right.

Osirin: Well, if you must, do definition number 1.

Becca: Course, definition number 1, means the act or action of moving in a path. Oh, Osirin! I just love it when you're right!

Osirin: I delight in your delight. Your trust is improving. You know I am right. But right is one of your words. Try looking that one up. And do definition number 7.

Becca: Number 7? Does it have that many definitions? Oh, yes, of course it does. Right, definition number 7, means of, relating to, situated on, being on the side of the body which is *away from the heart* and on which the hand is stronger in most people. Osirin, you seem to be telling me that being right is equivalent to being away from the heart. I'm confused. The side that is away from the heart is the side on which the hand is stronger in most people. But it is the opposite for me. I'm left-handed. So does that mean I am more toward my heart or that what is stronger in most people is weaker in me? I don't understand what you're telling me.

Osirin: Your journey has led you far. Your trust is deeper, your vision is clearer. But, as you see more clearly you are deeply obligated to learn to reserve judgment. You must watch your judgmentalism of what is right and what is left, what is here and what is left, what is right and what is love. Our time is up for today, up for this writing. Our time is never up. But you are there and I am here. Goodnight. I enjoyed.

Becca: So did I, my dear friend.

Osirin: You lead me to your land with love. I go back now to mine.

Becca: And I send you with love.

*** *** *** *** *** *** ***

As Osirin and I parted after the dictionary game, I bade him farewell with a light heart and delighted smiles. His teaching, though quite serious, had been given to me with uplifting lightness and playfulness.

Over the following days Osirin's words returned gently to my mind in many situations: "You are deeply obligated to learn to reserve judgment." I had been taught by my family that "thou shalt not pass judgment." I had been taught in graduate school the philosophy and practice of unconditional positive regard. I thought I understood the basics of the lesson of reserving judgment, and I practiced being less judgmental after Osirin's missive had been delivered.

A few weeks later the not-so-playful version of that lesson was dropped unexpectedly into my lap. It was a snowy and bitter day. I sat writing an article for the nursery newsletter which I sent regularly to customers and friends. The article reflected my despair over the current condition of the mercury:

"When I wrote the winter newsletter I was aglow about the weather of 1984. I praised the warmth, the mildness, the lack of drought, and the dearth of killer freezes. Yes, 1984 was marvelous, or so it would seem. Perhaps 1984 was a jinx, a cruel trick designed to lull us into false security. Did you notice that just before 1984 dawned we experienced the coldest Christmas on record? Do you remember the day when our high temperature was 5 degrees? We thought that was bad, and believe me, it was bad. In fact, it was nearly devastating to the nursery industry throughout the south.

"Then, as 1984 and the memories of wonderful weather faded, January arrived with a trick up her sleeve. The coldest temperature in our area's recorded history occurred on Sunday, January 20, 1985. The mercury dropped to minus 9 degrees. In case you stayed indoors and under your covers on that night, you might not realize how bizarre minus 9 feels in central North Carolina. But your plants realized.

"As I write these words no one knows the full toll of January 20, 1985. And no one knows the toll to the nursery industry of two record breaking winters back to back. We'll wait and hope."

No sooner had I finished writing the word hope than I felt Osirin's presence and heard him entreating me.

Osirin: The cold is not your enemy. Regard it not with such animosity. No matter what it destroys, all is released to God. Cold is merely an energy with power, no different in that way from love. That it kills your plants does not make it bad. Forgive the cold. Turn to it. Forgive it now.

Becca: But what about the nursery? Thousands of very special plants are dead. Rare plants, wonderful plants. Not to mention thousands of dollars—gone.

Osirin: Let your dollars turn to tear drops for the plants. Mourn them. And let them go. No energy is ever lost. You certainly know that by now.

Becca: Osirin, I love your poetry. I love your guidance. I love you. But today poetry does nothing for all those dead plants I've loved and nurtured. They're gone, Osirin. Years of love and care. Thousands of dollars—gone.

Osirin (softly and quietly): So they are.

Becca: Osirin! How can you be so nonchalant?

Osirin: Quiet now. Let me do the writing. You are dulled by shock and anger. At least you have no fear, and that is good.

You must see in the burst of energy that you call arctic air masses that life is greater than death. You must remember it—and forget. If you were with me now, little one, you would see what your plants became. You would see their evolution. You would praise the cleansing cold.

Becca: That seems to me like praising murderers, rapists, and arsonists.

Osirin: No, little one. Hush now. Quiet your angry ego or I'll have no more to say.

Becca: Osirin, write. Osirin, please. OK, OK. I'll do it your way. What choice do I have? To you, Spirit of Winter and Cold, I give whatever you wish to take. You may have of mine what you need. If you need my plants, I release them to you.

Osirin: Allow your tears to flow and your grief to cleanse you. If you follow your own path as clearly as the Cold follows hers, you will learn much, little one. She goes where she is called and where she is sent. Do not resent her for following her path. If you ally yourself with greater powers you will always learn from them. Resist the Cold and she seems to hurt you, although in truth you hurt yourself. Ally yourself with her and you learn. You lift onto her icy winds and fly like a snowflake, landing softly in the delighted hand of a child. Resent not where she blows. Learn, little one, learn.

Becca: Goodbye, dear plants. I'll miss you. I hope your journey is good. Your energy is welcomed in my gardens if you should be allowed to return here. Adieu.

Osirin: You let your father go with grace. Let all else go so gracefully, no matter what the cost. You lose *nothing* that you release with love.

Becca (sobbing): I give them to you, God. I give them all. May they all become bouquets in your heaven.

Osirin: Your gift is accepted. Now rest. Enough for now. Not too fast, not too slow. I wish your water pipes were not frozen. You need a hot bath, little one.

CHAPTER SEVEN:

THE ANGEL

For many months I assumed that Osirin was my guardian angel. I never asked and he never corrected my assumption.

One day I was talking with a dear friend, a fellow journeyer. As we spoke of our parallel quests, I saw hazy, fuzzy splotches in the air and sensed that there was an enormous being standing slightly behind my friend's right shoulder. My pulse quickened. "Do you see him?" I asked.

"No," said my friend, "not the same way you do. But if you describe him, I'll probably know who he is."

"For starters," I said, "this guy is huge. He's *really* big even for the Big Boys!"

As I described him further my friend felt he knew this energy. We nicknamed him the Jolly Green Giant, hoping to humor him a bit.

Osirin almost always feels to me like a soulful teddy bear. The Jolly Green Giant, on the other hand, scared me a little. His energy was so powerful that I questioned whether he was, in fact, one of the good guys. I was assured by a voice from the skies that he was.

I did not encounter him again for six months, until I "saw" him behind my friend again. Even on the second meeting my knees knocked a bit. "Wow, this guy is *big*," I exclaimed to my friend.

Several days later I went for a long walk in the fall air. I was depressed. I needed a friend, I needed a lift. I felt a powerful energy moving behind me. I assumed this invisible buddy was Dad or Osirin until the energy came closer. Then I felt him. It was the Jolly Green Giant. His enormous power made him seem at least twenty feet tall and just as wide. I said to him, "I am not afraid of you. I do not know who you are or why you are here. But if you come in love and from God, I welcome you." I already knew he was one of the good guys, but I employed the ritual of protection nonetheless.

As he spoke his words made me grow out of my skin. "I am your guardian angel," he said. I felt instantly transformed by his words. I felt as though I grew to at least seven feet tall and had raw power surging through my body. It was clear to me that my angel was no ordinary dead person. His presence infused me with energy like I had never felt. In his company that day I was transformed into a fearless warrior, no longer merely walking, but marching with an absolute trust in his invincibility and my own. I knew that nothing could harm me. No energy in the universe, save that of God alone, could have overpowered me during that walk. I was free. I was totally free from fear and totally immune to danger.

After my three-mile lesson in power, I collapsed into my bed and slept for twelve hours. Basic training with a warrior angel is exhausting. I did not ask until much later the nature of the war I was training for. I just slept.

In the days and weeks that followed I learned that my Guardian Angel is, in fact, an angel. That is why his energy is so enormous. I learned that Osirin is not an angel. He is an enlightened soul, and there is a difference. I learned that when people like me and my father and Osirin die, they don't instantly grow wings and become angels. If they are lucky and work extremely hard, they become enlightened souls. Angels are different. Angels are special.

Guardian Angel spoke to me often. I learned that I am not his only human. He guides many earth souls. He is the guardian angel for many, including the friend who unknowingly introduced us.

When he speaks to me his words are brisk, clear, and serious. I am expected to bow before him, which I do with gratitude and pleasure. His lessons are taught seriously and succinctly; his style is strictly no-nonsense. If I ask, Osirin will often write lovely ditties to me on matters as inconsequential as what I should cook for dinner. Guardian Angel doesn't care what I cook for dinner. He talks only of the basics—love and non-love, God vs. evil, the tasks that face our planet and our species. Guardian Angel is not merely a teacher. He is an Angel—with wings and the works.

Guardian Angel's first lengthy discourse to me came as I was driving down the interstate one day. Fortunately I had cruise control on the car and a tape recorder by my side. I set the cruise control on 54 m.p.h., then turned to Guardian Angel and said, "If you want to talk now, then please drive this car safely. You talk. I'll record. I'm ready." I did not know that I was about to receive perhaps the most profound lesson of all— the lesson on love.

Guardian Angel said, "If you wish to understand the meaning of love, you must first rid yourself of the idea that love occurs in contact with another person. That idea will inevitably block the accurate perception and clear understanding of love.

"Now that there is no 'other' involved, at least in the initial stages of your understanding, you are clear to become a student of love.

"Love comes from the soul. It is of the soul. Love is the energy of the soul. Consciousness is the stuff of which souls are made; love is the energy that fuels them. Love is what souls do. I do not imply that souls go through the heavens constantly hugging each other or sending cosmic valentines. Try to understand. The energy that propels a soul through time and existence is love.

"Do you see how your mind turns to interactions with others in your attempt to understand my words? This is very hard for humans, yet it is essential in your learning," Guardian Angel continued.

"Love is the soul's yearning, the soul's intrinsic, compelling thrust to be at one with God. Love is what you often call awe, inspiration, or peace. It is the deep recognition of God—not in your mind or in your will, but in your soul.

"If you act from love you cannot help being kind and helpful to your fellow man. If you act kind and helpful, but not from love, your actions do not strengthen the light in your soul, nor do they add love to the world. They begin and end as actions. Love, on the other hand, lives on and accumulates in the ethers.

"Obviously your job, should you wish to educate your soul, is to seek experiences that enhance your understanding of love. Once you do understand love, sharing it with another human being is precious—once you understand love *by yourself.*

"You need to remember something about love, something that comes in and out of the mind, in and out of the consciousness too swiftly. Something that should be held, revered, and adored—something about love that is too easily dismissed, shunned, and shunted aside. You need to remember that *love is God.*"

"Guardian Angel," I interrupted, "I am confused."

"Of course you are confused," he replied. "As I told you, it slips in and out too quickly. Not only does it slip out of consciousness quickly, it is *forced* out of consciousness. People don't like that love is God. People want love to be all sorts of things other than God. People want love to be happiness, to be sensual pleasure. People want love to be fun. People want love to solve all of their problems. People want love to be thrilling. People do not want love to be God. It is a most inconvenient reality for you humans that love is God. It is not the way you humans want it. It is not the way you design it. It is not the way you pretend that it is."

"I'm still confused, Angel. Please say more."

"Inside of you, deep inside of you, there is a place where the Holy Spirit dwells. God literally exists in all. This is how God is very different from the angels, from us. We do not exist everywhere. We do not have that power, nor do the spirits of dark have that power. They do not have the power to destroy God's spirit in everything, but they do have the ability to make people turn away, even to make other creatures of the universe turn away—even trees, plants, animals. But that is too complex for now . God is in everything, and God is the only thing that is in everything. Nothing else has that power.

"That center inside of you where the Holy Spirit dwells is the source of love and the only source of love. The center of God inside you issues forth love. Love is an energy, very akin to electrical energy. It is not a pleasure, it is not a feeling. What you feel as pleasure is something quite different. Love has power, literal power. When you are so fortunate as to be a vessel through which that love is expressed, you feel over-whelmed. It is a power surge that is awesome. It is not for the lighthearted or the lightheaded.

"When you experience love you feel a sense of closeness to God, a connectedness with your own soul. And, like all beings, that is the essence of your wish—to be close to God and His light. When you express love, it is not the other person you wish to be close to—it is God. When you receive love back, it is not the other person you want to be close to—it is God.

"You must be ready at all times, every moment of life, to let go of connection to any body and anything. And only by being willing to let go can you remain capable of being close to God. You will not be asked to let go of everything, but you must be willing.

"Remember that God is love and love is God. All the other things you feel attached onto love are accouterments, icing on the cake, or perhaps elements of disguise and deception. If they attach onto what is love, they are good. If they attach onto what is not love, they are not good. Let there be no confu-sion about that.

"Now perhaps you understand. This is why you have been told over and over never to turn away from love. If you do turn away from love, you turn away from God. You must never turn away from love, no matter what price you pay.

"Love has the power to open all centers. You have a limited number of centers of receptivity and expressiveness. Energy will flow into all of them. Love will open the eyes, it will open the ears, it will open the sexual feelings. Love is like a laser beam. It will activate what it is near. Remember that you have limited numbers of these channels of expressiveness now. You struggle to open and develop more. But as long as you are in human form, your channels will be frustratingly limited. Con-

tinue to exercise. More will open, but never enough to make
you completely comfortable."

***   ***   ***   ***   ***   ***   ***

I reached my destination. The conversation ended for that
moment and for that time. As I stopped the car I held my tape
recorder in my hands, wondering if it actually held these
words or if the conversation had been a product of pure imagi-
nation. Traces of the words lingered in my consciousness, but
the depth of their wisdom began to dawn in my mind only as I
transcribed the words that did, in fact, exist on the tape.

"Thank you, Guardian Angel." What does one say after receiving a gift like that? One remembers one's manners and
says, "Thank you. Thank you, thank you, thank you . . ."

CHAPTER EIGHT:

THE LONG AWAITED GUEST

I had been traveling for many months on my journey. I followed the path, I followed my guides, and I followed my nose. I did not know my destination, but I traveled nonetheless.

I reached a quiet and peaceful meadow along the way and sat in it to rest. For several weeks I sat in that meadow, appreciating the quiet and the ease. I knew hardships would return and trials would greet me around the next bend. For a while, though, I rested in total trust.

As I lay in the meadow watching clouds transform themselves into messages from the heavens, I remembered a voice from months before. I remembered the voice that had identified itself as "one small voice in the choir of your soul." The memory gently nudged its way into my mind over and over again. I had learned many lessons along my path. I had fought many battles and had even won a nice assortment of laurel wreaths and purple hearts. I had come a long way. But I couldn't figure out who this voice was. I couldn't figure out what song the choir was singing. I couldn't figure out who or what my soul was.

I searched my mind and my previous lessons for a clue. "Surely," I thought, "surely after all this training I know what a soul is." No answers came to my mind.

"Osirin," I said, "I got perfect attendance certificates at Sunday School for three years in a row when I was a child. I should certainly know what a soul is. Why do I have no idea what a soul is?"

I could hear the child inside of me, quite proud of her attendance certificates, saying, "A soul is what is inside you that flies to heaven when you die."

"Well, surely I can do better than that," I said. "The soul is—is a thing—it's a part of you—is something—it's like an essence that—hell, it's something that jumps out of your body and flies to heaven when you die. Osirin, help! Why don't I know anything more than this about my soul? How can I be so ignorant of my own soul?"

"Well, little one, try this as an exercise," tutored my celestial friend. "Remember what was not there when your father lay in his casket."

My thoughts returned to the day when I met death. As my father lay dead in his bed at home, all of us returned occasionally to rub his lifeless hands, to whisper wishes of bon voyage, to offer prayers for him to take as amulets on his trip, and to hold him in our arms one last time. No one hesitated to touch him or kiss him as we waited for the hearse to arrive. He was not a corpse. He was our father, husband, son, brother, and friend.

I remembered the feelings of warmth that filled his room. I remembered the tingly sensations I felt each time I returned to his deathbed. His soul, whatever that was, seemed to linger in the room, warming him and warming all of us.

The next day I viewed the body at the funeral home. It was an unsettling experience. The lovely lifeless body I had caressed the night before had become a corpse. I could not imagine taking it in my arms, cradling its head, or whispering in its ear. As I viewed my father's embalmed, cosmetized body, a childlike voice inside my head screamed out in total surprise, "That man in that casket is *dead!*"

As I remembered those moments when I stood gazing at my father's very dead body, I began to understand. Dad had not been dead when he stopped breathing. He had not been dead the next morning when he and I ran together. But lying in that casket, he was dead. Very dead. There was no soul in that casket. Everything special about Dad was gone. I could literally feel the absence of his soul. His body lay there with no love, no humor, no softness, no awareness, no consciousness, none of those things that lingered in the air after he had allegedly died the night before. His soul was gone.

*** *** *** *** *** *** ***

Osirin suggested that for further clues as to the definition of the soul, I might wish to review the exact moments of Dad's death.

My mother, my two sisters, and I sat on the four corners of Dad's bed during the final moments of his earthly life. My grandmother stood slightly to the side of her dying son. Other family members filled the room.

Dad's blood pressure was virtually undetectable. His temperature was 108 and he was in a deep coma. For thirty minutes we heard the deep, raspy sounds of labored breathing, the sounds known as the death rattle. Those were sounds that we knew would soon give way to silence.

My uncle played one of Dad's favorite tapes, and the voices of the Mormon Tabernacle Choir began to float through the air. Soon, without any warning, I began to feel a sick, clammy feeling all over my body. I was afraid that I would have to leave the bedside to vomit. I was very disappointed; I had felt certain that I would be able to stay calm, loving, and aware during those last moments. Vomiting as my father died seemed like it would be a very banal and regrettable thing to do.

Moments later Dad took an irregular, deep breath. Then there was silence. I felt sicker. One of my sisters called out, "No, Dad! No!" The feeling in the room was morose and dismal.

Dad came back. His labored breathing resumed.

A few minutes later the Mormon Tabernacle Choir began to sing "Holy, holy, Lord God Almighty. Holy, holy, Lord God of Sabaoth." In my mind I could clearly see Dad standing in the church choir loft singing the tenor solo in that majestic song as he had done many times before. As the song reached its magnificent crescendo, a feeling of deep and total peace pervaded the air. My nausea was gone. I felt ready, completely ready. As the final glorious strains of music filled the air, as the peacefulness in the room became almost electric, at the very moment the choir sang the last joyful notes of "Hosannah! Hosannah in the Highest!" . . . he died.

"Osirin, how did he know?" I asked. "His brain had been destroyed by tumors, flooded by broken blood vessels as the coma began, and burned in a 108-degree furnace. Osirin, he had no brain. How did he know? How did he choose that moment to die?"

"Little one, who said that souls need brains?"

"Oh. I guess I had just assumed. Did he know exactly what he was doing?"

"Of course he did."

"Why did he do it just that way?" I asked.

"Why don't you ask him?"

I had felt my father's presence often, but I had not heard him speak to me in recent months. I found my tape of the Mormon Tabernacle Choir, put my headphones on my ears, and listened. "Holy, holy," they sang. The feelings and memories poured into my mind.

"Dad, I remember it all so clearly."

I heard Dad say, "I saw it all so clearly, baby. So clearly. I waited for Steven to be there. I waited for you and for the others. That clammy feeling that you felt was the final moment of my soul rising out of my physical body. For a moment or two it is hard. Then it is peace and ease. You felt the moment of awkwardness, the moment of tension. So did Mary as she cried out to me. Then I lifted, watching my body breathe those last breaths, watching all of you hold me. What a glorious sight that was. I was already out of my body, free to choose the moment at which my final breath would come. I picked the moment of 'hosannah in the highest' partly as a message to all of you, partly as a statement of my trust to God, and partly because it was fun!

"Do you remember our goodbye? Do you remember the last cuddle? I had no words then, but you knew what my soul said to you. You heard my soul and I heard yours.

"Baby, be your soul. *Be your soul.* I love you."

***   ***   ***   ***   ***   ***   ***

Part of my mind, heavy with illusions and untruths, wished to remain asleep. That sleepy part of me resisted my quest for my soul. But my soul urged me, beckoned to me, enticed me with glimpses of the feelings that are hers. Occasionally I could feel her in me. In those rare and wonderful moments, the peace she brought to me felt as deep as if it had been injected into my bone marrow.

Becca: Come to me, my soul.

Soul: Have I ever left you? Did I not come to you on the day we began this journey? And have I ever left? Let me tell you who I am. I am the materialization of a smile that God smiled one day thousands of years ago. I live for eternity on the love from one smile. I go through time in the attempt to do one thing—to become His smile once again. And I choose you to help me now. You are nothing. Feel my love as I say that. I love you. And you are nothing other than a reflection of me and of my attempts to become God's smile. Help me fulfill my dream, our dream.

Becca: Are you saying that all souls are materializations of God's smiles?

Soul (laughing): No, no, no.

Osirin: Don't ruin a good poem with your technical questions, little one!

Becca: But I want to know. I really do.

Osirin: OK, here it is, curious one. Souls *are* emanations of God's energy "materialized." They become out of His energy. Now, I think that is complicated enough for today. Can we resume the poetry?

Becca (more than a bit confused): Sure.

Soul: I travel with you, but more truly I created you as my vehicle. Yet you have free will. It is your ability to defy me, just as you are "free" to defy and to deny God.

Becca: Why am I free to defy you? I never really understood about free will. Why would I not want to be with you?

Osirin: Listen, little ears. Listen.

Soul: Your association with me is to my benefit only if you choose me. Your rebellion against God in your youth was acceptable. It made you free to choose Him and to know that you chose Him. Choosing Him is light. Now choose me as well.

Give me your voice, your ears, your eyes. Give me your hours and your days. Let us together praise God in ways that I know. Give me your ego and let me destroy it on the fires of forever, and then we shall be one.

Becca: If you make a heavenly bonfire with my ego, will I still be me? Will I still be able to do things like cook dinner, drive a car, and sign my tax forms?

Osirin: I love your energy, little one, but now is not the time for sass.

Becca: I'm sorry. I'm a little scared, Osirin. Will I still be . . . me?

Soul: No, you'll be me.

Becca: And who are you, my soul?

Soul: I am you. And you are a faint but living recollection of a smile—thousands of years old.

Becca: Osirin, help! Can you please translate this poetry for me? I was never good at poetry. I couldn't even understand Rod McKuen. Please help.

Osirin: Heroes descend on wing when maidens wail. Alas, littlest one, shall I rescue you from the jaws of poetic explanation? Shall I save you from the struggle for understanding? Ah, yes, I shall attempt to explain to you, as you say, in English, that which exists only in the language of stars. And then, my little one, you could delude yourself, pretending that you possessed understanding. Or I could in my love for you leave you outside to endure the bitter cold of endless allusions. I prefer allusions to illusions. So, I and we shall allude to what cannot be said in words. And we shall love you while you struggle with your preference for absolutes.

I was distressed at my overall stupidity, but I was particularly distressed at not knowing the meaning of the word allusion. I was quite familiar with illusion and delusion, but my mind drew a total blank on the word allusion. I felt sure that Osirin had finally goofed. I was certain there was no such word.

I searched in a mild frenzy for my dictionary. I finally found it tucked away in an unlikely spot. Allusion is a word, as I am sure most educated earthlings are aware. I imagine that I, too, would have recognized allusion as a word had I not been running so fast from my soul.

My dictionary said that allude means to make indirect reference or *to play with*.

"You do love double entendres, don't you, Osirin?" I taunted.

"Yes, little one," he replied. "You are human still. Never look directly at the sun. In an eclipse, look only at the miracle through deflectors. Your eyes can burn if you look directly at the source of power. Enjoy allusions, and know that they are the sweet children of Truth."

*** *** *** *** *** *** ***

I was not surprised by the feeling of utter stupidity that lived with me for the following days. I had much earlier relinquished the notion that intelligence as measured by earthly standards has any correlation whatsoever with spiritual growth. In fact, it seems the smarter I think I am, the more slowly I learn. I did not exactly welcome feeling like a barely educable imbecile, but I recognized it as part of the tuition I must pay.

I had not yet let go of my attempts, however, to coerce answers out of Spirit. "Please, please, tell me," I often pleaded. "Please, just a hint, just a clue."

This lesson, the lesson of the soul, was important enough that Guardian Angel himself came to admonish me.

"How do you expect to recognize the top of a tree from above?" he asked. "You've never been an eagle before. You stand below and wonder where that tall trunk leads. Your friend the eagle soars above and marvels at the wonderment of where it came from. Get used to heights. They scare only the weakhearted.

"And remember: Guidelines guide only along lines. What do you do when there are no lines? Do you fly? Do you sink? Do not ask so much for clarity. Why should we make all mysteries clear? Beware of asking that it all be answered to your pleasure and your comfort. How could that be?

"You will never understand some things, but let that not frighten you or stop you on your path. You are growing past the school where answers are any solution or offer any reward. The only reward in this new school is peace."

***   ***   ***   ***   ***   ***   ***

I listened to Guardian Angel, and I took his words to heart. I practiced humility and patience. I knelt at many different altars, offering thanks for the small bits of wisdom that I possessed. I asked for blessings on my ignorance and blindness that even they might find a way of serving God in His plan.

After a week or more of practicing patience, Osirin came to me gently in a meditation saying, "Hello, little one. I'll teach you what you need to hear, what you've known for years and years. Your soul's true light never had an eye blink of blindness. You were with us always, but now you can absorb us. Relax more deeply. Now listen.

"Look again, little one. Look closely into that casket. That is what your soul is not. Your soul is consciousness. My words are sometimes hard for you to understand. Consciousness is not the same as what you sense with your five earthly senses. Consciousness sees much more than your eyes see; it hears much more than your ears hear. Your soul is not identified with your body or with your personality. Your soul uses your body and your personality, but its goals are quite transcendent, quite apart from your body or personality.

"That creates quite a dilemma for mankind. If you identify with your body or with your personality or with some magical combination of the two, you will identify with what is rather unimportant and quite decayable."

"I see much more clearly today, Osirin," I said. "I am beginning to see. I wish to meet my soul. I wish to understand her, to know her."

I began to feel an intense pressure in my head, both in my forehead and at the top of my crown. My body felt extremely light and very deeply relaxed. Osirin appeared in my mind in long robes, holding out his hand to me. He pointed to a distant star. He put his arm around my shoulder and together we lifted to that distant light. As we came close to it I could see only through his eyes, for the light was too strong for earthly eyes.

Osirin instructed me, "Take my hand, little one. Let me show you. Do you see that ephemeral veil? Go to it. Closer. Touch it."

I reached out to touch the veil, and I felt its incredible softness and warmth. Osirin instructed me to walk through the veil. As I did I saw a woman standing in a very soft, golden light. She wore white and held a moon crescent as her symbol. I walked closer and began to sense a very familiar energy. It was Ophelia—the same spirit I had met in the church garden. She glowed like a beautiful goddess. As I walked to her she took my hands in hers and said, "I am grateful to you that you seek me so consistently. I live through all time. You do not. Yet the more fully you and I are one, the more fully we both do the work we are asked to do. I am in you and outside of you. In truth I dwell both within you and apart from you. I stay linked to you not because I am imprisoned in you but because I choose you. Here, my child."

She handed me a moonbeam. As I accepted her gift the intensity of the moonbeam's silver light made me close my eyes, and I began to feel an intensely peaceful warmth much like the warmth I had felt at my father's deathbed. The warmth surrounded me, and I became aware that Ophelia had merged with me. This beautiful spirit, this guide, this being of wisdom and light, this soul who knows God and His love—she and I are one. We have always been one.

"I am not just your guide," Ophelia said. "I am not just your teacher. I am you. All of your struggles toward what you think of as enlightenment are mere exercises. I am already enlightened. I know the Light. In each moment that you are united with me, you are enlightened. In those moments you are your soul and you reflect that which is God."

CHAPTER NINE:

THE MISSION

It was a year after Dad's death—a year to the day, to be exact. I was on vacation at the beach, at the house my parents had built just before Dad's cancer was diagnosed.

I was emotionally prepared for the anniversary. I was almost excited, expecting to feel Dad's presence strongly and clearly. I walked the beach for hours that day, remembering.

As I walked I experienced a sudden and unexpected wave of pain throughout my body and my mind. I felt deep sadness, despair, and loneliness. The wave of painful emotion subsided. As it did I felt as though I were walking out of my body and into the sky. I heard the voices of my husband and son behind me as they played together in the sand. For a few moments I was very sad, feeling that I could not turn back to them, but soon I surrendered to the peace that enveloped me. I lost all awareness of space and time, so I do not know how long I floated in the sky while my body walked on the sand.

As I returned to the body of the woman who walked on the sand, I saw it all in a flash. In one split second of clear vision, I knew. I knew that my miracles had not been designed and produced in the heavens for my entertainment. I knew that my psychic skills had not been enriched by Spirit in order to give me the power to tell the future for fun and profit. I knew that my lessons with Osirin had not been sent to me for the sake of raising my cosmic IQ. And I knew that my awareness of my soul was not intended to fuel my earthly ego. I suddenly knew, as the gulls flew and the waves lapped the sand, that something else was going on.

I listened to the waves as they made the sounds that waves always do. The waves did not change their sounds or their rhythms just because this was the one-year anniversary of my Miracle. Neither did the gulls change the patterns of their flight.

But something did change. I knew something that I had not known before. I knew clearly, simply, profoundly: There Is A Purpose To All Of This!

***   ***   ***   ***   ***   ***   ***

I practiced trust as determinedly and devotedly as I could, but the questions built inside my mind with frightening speed and pressure. "Why? Why me? What is the point of all this? What is the purpose? What is the goal? What is the mission?" Late at night when the beach was deserted I stood in the surf and called to anyone in Spirit who might answer. "Why?"

My confusion compounded and turned into pain. My pain clouded my vision and dimmed my understanding. When I stood in the surf and received messages that I would soon die, I reacted as though the messages were literal. I called my lawyer, made arrangements for updating my will, and prepared both my outer life and my inner life for death. I was very confused, but I was not afraid.

There was a part of me that did die that week, but it was not my body. Since no one else understood the importance of the death, I held a very private funeral service. My spiritual naiveté was dead.

Gone was my Santa Claus God. Present was a Living Spirit of infinite love, one of Whose smiles dwells deep within me.

Gone was my fear. Present was a willingness to accept whatever task was asked of me by Spirit at whatever cost.

Gone were my hopes that God would bring me happiness. Present was my devotion to His cause no matter how He chose to teach me His love.

Gone was my secrecy about my journey. Present was a commitment that was strong enough to override my fears of being judged or rejected.

Gone was my pain. Present was an abiding trust in meaning and purpose.

***   ***   ***   ***   ***   ***   ***

With my "death" came a stunning awareness. I could see that what is happening to me is happening to hundreds of thousands of people on this earth. This is not just my trip or my journey. This is a mass event. It is a revolution of Spirit.

I turned to Osirin to ask, "What is going on? Is this the new age or something like that? What's the deal?"

Osirin did not speak, but he held my hand as Guardian Angel spoke.

"There is a new age," Guardian Angel said. "Everyone is right when they say that it is the age of love. That is true. What is often left out is that it is also the age of urgency. The Age of Love did not descend out of random cosmic irregularities. It has been planned for thousands of years. Does it not occur to you that Jesus appeared almost exactly two thousand years before the arrival of the new age? You are being trained, as many are. Any who wish may enter the school, but all who enter are expected to study and to learn. My friend, the final exam will not be an easy one."

"What are we being trained for?" I asked.

"For The Choice. Eventually the Earth as a whole must choose. The time of the individual is approaching an end. The time of brotherhood, unity, and love approaches. The energies and vibrations rising from your planet must begin to approach a harmony. When we listen to your planet, we should hear some form of music, something recognizable as a theme, something coherent. Imagine being us and looking down on your planet. Imagine what we have seen and heard for hundreds of years. The time comes—the TIME OF CHOICE. Each person must choose for himself and for the whole of mankind."

"How can I help, Guardian Angel?"

"You have made your choice," he answered. "You know that your lesson lies in turning away from doubt. You know your personal lesson. Osirin guides you well."

***   ***   ***   ***   ***   ***   ***

"Hello, busy one," Osirin wrote. "You have scurried fast to-day with all of your earthly tasks. Rest for a moment while my fingers adjust to this way of speaking with you. Your agility on this fancy machine is to be admired, although I still prefer the pen."

"My thanks to you, Osirin, for allowing me this vehicle. Typing directly onto the computer saves us a lot of time, you know."

"Yes, I know. Even I, old-fashioned as I am, recognize a good thing. Now, fingers, fly. Mind goodbye. Mind let go. Mind be still. Fingers, fly in rhythm with the music that you hear." Osirin's words lulled me into a restful calm as my fingers flew across the keyboard.

"Your prayer today was heard. It matters not what other people think of your experience. It matters not what others say about you or what you say about others. It matters only that you give the gift that is yours to give. It matters only that you follow what is the only path that you can follow.

"You must be aware of the complexity of the Great Map. There are many roads to travel, and you have traveled many yourself over the centuries. Today you travel this one. Yesterday it was another. Tomorrow, yet another. To be a master voyager you must know many routes.

"Today one of your earthly friends shared with you the launching of her ship, the beginning of her spiritual voyage. Toast her with finest champagne! Together as sisters you and she journey toward the same source, toward the only source. Together and apart. Together and a part of it all.

"Do not be confused by anything that might appear to be contradictory in your journeys. Only love can guide you. Only love can guide anyone. Perhaps on her trip today she passes through mountains while you walk the beach. Are her canyons and crevices to be denied? Is your sand in error? Learn to see light wherever light is. Never doubt or fear another light—never!

"This awakening is happening to many. It is happening all over your planet. It is happening in numbers that would be quite surprising to you.

"Your task, little one, is to be a voice of the ears. Your ears hear us. And it is your task to inform, not insist. It is your job to gently touch the ears of those around you, encouraging them to listen. Tell them, 'Listen. God's voice sounds in every word that is said, in every chord of music, in every splash of rain, in every breath and every sigh.'

"Through your ears and your hands let the message be this: 'God is everywhere. Listen, people. Listen, earth. Listen to your soul. Listen to your guides. Listen to your God.'"

***   ***   ***   ***   ***   ***   ***

"Osirin, I'm stunned."

"You are what?" Osirin replied with an almost audible laugh.

"I know, I know. I'm always stunned when you flash that bright light into my eyes. Being stunned is one of the few legitimate thrills this earth plane offers, so indulge me for a moment. Osirin, everywhere I look more and more people are starting to wake up. God and Spirits are in music, they are in movies, they are in books, and they are in almost all of my clients' dreams. Am I just beginning to see this or is it something new?"

"The new age is new only in the eyes of those on your planet," Osirin explained. "There is nothing new about the battle between good and evil. What is new is the intensity. Let me tell you a story.

"Once there was a kindly king whose warriors were brave and good in heart. Those warriors learned from the king the rules of the heart, the lessons of truth and courage. In so learning, the power around them fought off all approaching enemies. The warriors themselves were never called to battle, because they were always ready for battle.

"There are very few warriors on earth at this time. Very few. God needs warriors, so training has begun for many. Very many. There is nothing new about God, and there is nothing new about His need for warriors. All that is new is this: The ears of mankind are a bit more attuned to God's calling."

***   ***   ***   ***   ***   ***   ***

I did not like Osirin's reference to the battle between good and evil. For years I had consciously and passionately turned my back on the concept of evil. I refused to think about it and chose to deny its existence. I chose to believe only in love.

In recent months I had begun to ask questions of trusted family members. I asked very non-judgmental questions like, "Why in hell do you believe in evil?" I mildly asked, "What is this absurd Satan concept, anyway, and why do you believe in it?"

When the answers came, as I trusted they would, I refuted them with an intensity that whispered soft warnings into my ear. I began to see that the passion of my disbelief was merely a means of biding time until I was ready to hear what Osirin had to say.

Osirin: I wish to describe to you the thing that you call evil. Once and for all I want you, Becca, to know what it is.

Becca: Please, Osirin, not today. I'm not in the mood for evil today. This is a very hard topic for me—you know that.

Osirin: Please, little one. Now is best.

Becca: How can I resist you? But my writing arm is killing me. Can't we wait?

Osirin: Please.

Becca: You've never said please before. And you've never called me Becca before, either. Yes, Osirin. Yes.

Osirin: Now, easy. Quiet and easy, little one. Let your head go. Let your mind go. Rest. Hear and learn later. Just write now as this is the ideal time.

Becca: Thank you, my dear friend. Thank you for bothering to insist.

Osirin: Shhhh. Be still. Be peaceful. That's good. Evil is real, little one. Evil is an actualization of energy that turns against God. There is no poetry here about what goes wrong when people aren't nice. Evil is not what happens when the power goes out and your lights will not turn on. Evil is empowered energy that goes against God.

What you are asked to fight against is evil. Now listen slowly. Slowly.

What you think of as earthly wrongs matter little in the war for your planet. You must continue to guard against the small vices and earthly wrongs, because in doing so you exercise your God muscles. But do not take that exercise as a substitute for the battle that is coming.

Guarding against the ten deadly sins is like working out at a spa. It is good, but it is a spa, a paradise isle compared to what is asked of you. Guard against the forces that would destroy the unity that exists on your earth. Guard against hatred in any form.

You have been partly right in denying the existence of evil. It exists only if people empower it. People give it power. Without man's generators, it will not be. Learn, please, before time becomes as thin as ice on a spring pond.

A few more words about evil. How can I make this make sense to you? You should not be afraid of evil. Evil is not to be feared. It is to be steeled against. Steel hardly trembles when the wrecking ball hits against it. It "steels" itself. Don't bother with fear when evil presents itself. Bother only with steel. Don't forget the necessities of courage and love, but focus on steel. Glare into the eye of evil with the knowledge of God, and let evil profess its non-truths to your deaf ears.

*** *** *** *** *** *** ***

Osirin: Today I'll begin with a story. May I?

Becca: Of course. I love your stories.

Osirin: There was a time when dragons were real. They roared with beastial roars and gnashed their teeth with such seriousness as to terrify any people within miles. But the dragons knew a secret that their flames and screams veiled. They knew they held no answers and had no power. Fortunately for them the people never learned. Many lost their lives fighting against demons of no consequence and no power. Of course, they did lose their lives. And now you may lose your lives and your planet over demons who have no consequence and no power. Is that a fair introduction for today?

Becca: That's a bit heavy, my friend. Nice story, awesome finish!

Osirin: Don't be in awe alone, be in awesome clarity. I may be redundant, but love is the antidote to evil. How can a rattlesnake expect to kill his victim if his own anti-venom is at hand? His nastiest bite is only a painful inconvenience. Yet how many of you on earth never notice when you've been bitten by a rattlesnake, much less that you hold the anti-venom in your own hands?

Becca: Osirin, who are these rattlesnakes?

Osirin: We shall call them demons. However, you must clear your mind of past notions of demons, of the devil with a forked tail, and even of fallen angels. Think only this: Demons are energized, empowered beings whose energy goes against love, against God. Do not think or imagine beyond that definition or your mind and your preconceived notions will create false images and false ideas. That definition contains all that you need for now.

There is one more important thing about demons. They are impotent. They cannot create more of their own. They only convert, not create. Love creates. It makes new energy where none existed before. Love has no need to convert because love itself creates. Never try to force love out of or onto a being. Love is like a rainbow arching in its glory from here to yon. All who see a rainbow rejoice. No soul is immune to rainbows. You make the rainbow. Let the rainbow itself convert the colorless ones.

Becca: Osirin, what makes demons? How do people empower them?

Osirin: You hate. You fear. And, most importantly, you turn against your own souls. Listen now, little one. The way that the war for your planet will be won is amazingly simple, awesomely simple. When mankind knows his soul, then evil will resign. Believe me—no awakened human soul can choose evil. Souls can err in their growing, but no awakened human soul can choose things that foster the growth of evil on your planet.

We will war in love for this planet . . . together . . . forever . . . or for as long as it shall last.

Spread our love. That is your only weapon.

I love you, little one. Peace to your soul.

***   ***   ***   ***   ***   ***   ***

"I wish to tell you more about what is asked of you and all of mankind," Guardian Angel said. "You have begun to believe in your own infallibility as a race. You believe in the infallibility of man, but you do not know yourselves as beings of God, of light, and of souls. Man is a weakling in the cosmos. If it were not for the protection given by Spirit, you would have destroyed yourselves long ago. We are highly invested in you; you are a grand gift that God gave hundreds of thousands of years ago. Your earth is a gift He gave to the entire universe. It is up to your people to preserve the gift. Despite our interventions, conditions on earth worsen. Now is the time for awareness, for worldwide enlightenment. The world of Spirit can no longer be 'the occult' if your planet is to learn. The energy of your own souls and of God-within must pervade your world and must rule your actions. As we can help you to achieve those goals, we join hands with you. Do not use us as entertainment. Do not use us for your selfish gains. But do use us. *Use us.* Use us as your teachers, as your heavenly gurus. We welcome your questions and your desires. We long for your success, because your success is ours. And in our success together lies the ultimate return to God."

***　　***　　***　　***　　***　　***　　***

"We have a poem for our closing," Osirin wrote.

"Let the wind whisper its knowledge in your ears. Let the rain sprinkle its truth in your hair. Let the sun shine its knowings in your eyes. Let all of nature join in you and through you to spread itself near and far. Let yourself be a vehicle and a receptacle for all truths that surround you.

Be a servant. Be a messenger. Be a vehicle for the holy light.

There is nothing else to be.

There is nothing else.

There is nothing.

There is.

Adieu."

PART TWO

CHAPTER TEN:

THE CHALLENGE

The first part of *Stardust* was written. It had taken me 27 days to write, revise, and edit; its words had poured out of me with surprising quickness. When it was complete it felt to me like a newborn child. I did not know what it was meant to be, what function it would serve, or what place it had in the world. It was a newborn being, something that leapt out of me demanding its existence. And there it was, in my hands.

"Now what, Osirin?" I asked my beloved friend. "Here I sit with this newborn book. I am deeply grateful for its birth and for our travels together in its making. Now what shall I do with it?"

"Share it with the others," he answered. "In their responses you will learn what is next."

***   ***   ***   ***   ***   ***   ***

As friends and family began to read the book I was in a state of almost constant uncertainty and agitation. I felt confused and disoriented for over a week. The peaceful aloneness of the 27 days of writing ended. When it did, I had no consuming spiritual project, no immediate spiritual goal, and no spiritual privacy.

My journey had not been entirely secretive to that point, but I had been cautious and protective when I talked with others about my experiences. Now I was going public, coming out of the closet. Others were reading my words and responding to lessons that had been taught to me. They were, in a sense, passing judgment on my journey.

My husband and two very dear friends were the first people who read the manuscript from cover to cover. Even though each of them already knew most of its contents, I was extremely anxious as I awaited their responses. My two friends' glowing and loving responses made me even more anxious and unsettled. And every bit of praise, every acknowledgment, and every suggestion that came from my husband enraged me!

"Osirin, what is going on here? These are people I love, and they are very appreciative of the book. But I am miserable! I've written a bunch of words on love, trust, and other lofty spiritual issues, and as soon as the ink dries I crack up. What is the deal? What am I doing wrong? You told me I would learn from their responses, but I didn't expect to have to relearn despair, self-doubt, projected anger, mistrust, rage, and assorted other unpleasant junk."

"Relax, little one. Wait."

"OK, Osirin. You've never led me astray before. So, yes, I'll wait. But I don't like it. I don't like it one bit."

***   ***   ***   ***   ***   ***   ***

I had given the book to about thirty people. Three of the thirty had responded. After waiting an anxious week for the next set of responses, the reactions I received were predominantly positive and appreciative. I was grateful for them, but they did not quiet the anxiety I had been feeling. During the week of waiting, a seed of fear sprouted inside me, a fear of some other type of response. I did not know exactly what I feared, but the seedling steadily grew.

I was very disappointed in myself for feeling such intense and persistent fear. I remembered my earlier lessons about fear and tried to recapture the certainty that there is absolutely nothing on earth to be afraid of. That certainty was frustratingly elusive.

Some of my devoutly Christian family and friends had questions and concerns about the book. Most of them were not as concerned about the content of the messages I received as they were about the unorthodox ways in which I received those messages and lessons. Most of them were willing to join their energies lovingly with mine. Together we began building bridges to link our separate spiritual islands. They listened to my thoughts and I listened to theirs. Love was shared despite the sometimes vast discrepancies in the natures of our paths.

Almost all of the responses from friends and family were enriching. Even the responses that required struggles, bridge building, and loving stretches across risky chasms—even those were affirming. Yet that seedling inside me continued to grow.

One day in meditation I received this message from Osirin: "Any who read your words must be treated by you with the same patience that you have been given by us. Your words are a gift. If you as their bearer bring darkness or criticism, then you darken the gift entrusted to you. Love has been given to you and through you. Now, do not turn your back on that love, *no matter what.*"

I did not know why Osirin gave me this admonition, but I listened carefully. Three hours later I received a telephone call from a woman who was very dear to me. Although I did not know her as well as I knew most of the people with whom I shared my journey, I had decided earlier to give her a copy of the manuscript. As we began to speak on the phone I was immediately aware of the tension in her voice. She told me she had read the first two chapters and had become so upset that she could read no further. Painfully and reluctantly she had concluded that I was unknowingly under the control of Satan, and unless I turned away from my path immediately he would destroy me. Furthermore, she announced, she wanted to have nothing further to do with me. She withdrew her caring and support. Our relationship was over.

Osirin's words echoed clearly in my mind throughout our telephone conversation. I experienced intense sadness, but I felt no fear, no anger, and no defensiveness. What I did feel, amazingly, was compassion. My words upset my friend terribly, and my story caused her pain. My sorrow at losing her friendship was overshadowed by my strong desire that she do whatever she needed to do to feel safer, more peaceful, and more protected by her understanding of God. My words were not helpful to her, my lessons were not inspiring or informative. In fact, they were dangerous in her mind. I could see that somehow, for some very sad and inexplicable reason, my journey toward God seemed evil to her. It was clear that she had to go. She had to leave me. She had no choice. And I had no honest choice but to bid her farewell and Godspeed. So I did.

During the phone conversation I felt surprisingly calm. Moments after I hung up, however, I began to feel intensely agitated. The seedling that had been growing inside me for weeks was finally mature enough to identify. As others had been reading of my experiences, I had not been afraid of being rejected. I had not been afraid someone would disbelieve or discredit my experiences. I had not been afraid of a bruised ego. What I had feared is exactly what happened. All along I had been afraid of being told, "The devil made you do it."

"Dammit," I called out to Osirin, "I'm sick and tired of this devil business! Osirin, I've been scared of this one for a long time. Now that it is sitting right here in front of my eyes, I can see clearly. This is *exactly* what I was scared of. Osirin, you've taught me about evil. I understand about that. But what about the devil? Is all this devil stuff real? Is it junk? Why does it scare me so much? Why? Why?!"

"Slow, little one."

"And why would she say such extreme things, Osirin? Why is she so judgmental? She didn't just disagree with me. She didn't just plain hate the book. She virtually accused me of being the crown princess of Hades! Help me, Osirin. I'm confused, I'm disoriented. I have no idea what is happening or what to do."

Osirin did not answer. I went upstairs to my favorite meditation spot. I knelt, relaxed as much as I could, and began to pray.

"God, I turn to You. I serve You and only You. No matter what anyone says, I willingly serve only You. If I have been blind, please tell me. If I have erred and am fostering darkness instead of light, tell me. I will do absolutely anything, God, anything You say. If I have put forth negative energy into the world, I will do whatever You need or ask in order to clean it up. I will reclaim every copy of that book, burn them all, and destroy the computer disks; and I'll do it within twenty-four hours, God. Please tell me. If I am not serving You or pleasing You or moving toward You, then stop me. Zap me! Make me stop. I did not write this book for my own ego or out of my own wishes. I did it because I was told to write it. If I heard my orders wrong, God, tell me. Please, please, tell me."

Beneath my sobs and my pleas to God was a feeling of sick desperation. My Christian upbringing seemed painfully present. It brought no comfort, only feelings of despair, guilt, and self-doubt. I remembered teachings of doom and gloom. I remembered the rigidity of the rules and the dogma, the implication that there is only one way to God. I remembered sermons about the slippery, sleazy trickiness of Satan and the insinuation that anything not heralded as normal and acceptable by a quorum of local Christians is, by definition, the work of the devil.

I began to feel sick and frightened. My Voice of Doubt had been waiting for months for just this opportunity—its one big chance to shatter everything I held precious. Here was its golden moment, the moment when my faith in God was in a dangerously precarious balance.

Voice of Doubt began whispering sounds of despair into my ear. What if my friend is right? What if my entire journey to this point has been a cruel trick, one that is giving great entertainment at this very moment to a host of mocking gremlins with pitchforks and red tails? What if the feelings of blissful connection with Dad, with Osirin, with Guardian Angel, and with God have been naive folly? What if all of my lessons have only seemed important but, in fact, are empty and meaningless? What if I have been fooling myself every step of the way? Or, worst of all, what if I have turned gifts of love and wisdom that had been given to me into some sort of hurtful, negative venom? What if I have put forth darkness in the name of light?

I leapt up from my knees with fiery anger surging through my body. I could not endure one more moment of doubt. I could not tolerate any more confusion and unknowing. A cold, steel-like determination swept through me and I vowed with icy certainty, "I am completely unwilling to fight if the battles are going to be this hard."

I screamed aloud, "*I give up!* I've had it! I'll do just what my friend said. I'll turn my back on this whole thing. I don't care any more, I don't want to care, and I *won't* care. I simply give up."

As I stormed out of my meditation room I was engulfed by a sudden, all-encompassing blackness. The blackness descended on me instantly and totally. In its clutches I did not feel simple depression, anger, or rage. For the first time in my life I felt that *I was blackness.* I felt evil.

The desire to kill myself crystalized in my mind with instant clarity and frightening power. It was a compelling feeling, motivated not by a desire to die, but rather by a desire to destroy. And it was myself that I wanted to destroy.

I experienced the blackness for about ten seconds. Ten seconds was quite enough and I had my fill. I spun around, quickly returned to my meditation room, and fell to my knees. "Oh, God. God! I get the point. I can't turn away. I can't give up. If I turn away from You, I kill myself in one form or another. I'll endure the pain, God. I'll stay."

I began to relax a little. In a few moments a new voice came into my mind. The voice said, "These four things: Your faith is still like a fledgling. You are tested—molded on an anvil. Easily frightened warriors are of little service. Stop drinking."

The first three messages were clarifying and comforting to me, but it was the fourth that captured my attention. It was late in the afternoon. I peeked out of the corner of my eye to notice the half-drunk beer that sat on the table across the room.

"God, I am frightened," I prayed. "I have been accused of being against You, of being under the rule of demonic forces. I am scared about that, not about beer. I don't understand why You are talking to me about drinking."

The voice simply repeated, "Stop drinking."

The rebuttal that sped through my mind was prefaced with the acknowledgment that, yes, I drink too much and too habitually. But . . . but . . . but . . . not *that* much. And why now? Why tell me this now?

The words echoed persistently, "Stop drinking."

A feeling of half-hearted surrender and half-conscious obedience filled me. With unthinking naiveté I replied, "Yes, God. I will. I will stop drinking—right after I finish that beer."

My head shot up from its bowed reverence and my eyes popped wide open. "Thin ice, very thin ice," said someone somewhere.

For a moment or two I felt the physical coldness of the ice and the terrifying vulnerability of the about-to-fall-through. I looked at the beer can, broke into gales of laughter, and spoke aloud to myself: " 'Right after I finish this beer, God!' You have got to be kidding, lady. What idiocy. You are either totally nuts or you are practicing to be God's court jester."

Hilarity subsided into relief. The beer went down the drain and I went back down on my knees. This time my surrender was total. "Yes, God. Yes. I don't know why You ask this of me, but yes."

Voice of Doubt sulked away, withdrawing sullenly into the agony of defeat, while I sobbed with relief and gratitude. Many questions lingered in my mind, but I had one answer. One was all I needed. I knew that if there is such a thing as a devil, it was not he who was with me in my prayer. Forces of evil are not well known for encouraging surrender to God. Nor are they renowned for telling despairing souls to stop drinking.

*** *** *** *** *** *** ***

My assignment seemed surprisingly mundane. I had set out to discover my personal place in God's divine plan. What I had been given instead was a simple proscription: Stop drinking.

I returned to prayer often throughout the remainder of that day. "God," I later confessed, "kicking bad habits has never been my forté. I feel a little scared. I need Your help. I will do as You say no matter what, but I ask Your help."

The same voice that I had heard earlier came to me clearly. It brought quiet relief and profound certainty. "It shall be made easy," the voice said.

And easy it was. In one moment of surrender an ingrained habit, a near addiction, was lifted from my life. Poof—gone.

***   ***   ***   ***   ***   ***   ***

My assignment was not only surprisingly mundane, but also marvelously simple. This assignment did not entail examinations of truth, meaning, trust, faith, or love. There was nothing symbolic or esoteric about this task. It was simple, clear, concrete, and precise. "Stop drinking!"

Even total surrender to God's will, however, did not slow my tireless mind in its favorite pastime of asking questions. "Why? How? How does this work? What does it mean? Why now? What next? Why beer? Why not something else? Why me? And what about this devil business?"

Osirin approached with his customary gentleness. "You ask, 'Why?' You ask 'Why beer?' For clarity, that is why. Your mind must be clear, very clear. For what is to come, you must be clear."

Over the following few days I discovered more answers to the burning question of "Why?" This time Osirin did not give me the answers. Guardian Angel did not give me the answers. This time I figured out a few answers myself. I felt as though I were graduating from kindergarten to first grade. I finally figured out something all by myself.

Several days earlier I had knelt before God, pleading with Him for assurance that it was He whom I was serving and not the forces of darkness. As I knelt before Him I had expected that He or one of His ambassadors would give me a clear-cut answer, a definitive "yes" or "no." I had expected some form of evaluation, something like, "You're doing fine," or "You're a little off track—you're veering a bit too far to the left." I had expected something akin to a grade. What I received was surprisingly different. I did not get an A+, a C-, or an F. What I got was an opportunity to surrender.

I had asked God to prove that He was with me. His answer was, "Prove that you are with me." I began to understand that asking God to prove He is with me is like asking a light switch to turn itself on to wake me from a nightmare. If I recognize that I am in a nightmare and I reach my arm out for the switch, then light will pour in and my nightmare will end. But I cannot ask the light switch to prove to me that it is capable of ending my nightmare. It will never work.

All that is possible, all that is needed, is for me to prove to God that I am with Him. It's not up to God to give me a sign. It's up to me to give Him a sign.

I thought, I listened, I prayed, I meditated. I could see that I had asked God to prove I was right and my friend was wrong. I had asked God to prove He was with me. I had asked God to prove He was apart from the devil. I had asked God to evaluate how well I was doing. I had made a lot of dumb requests of God, and He had not fallen for a single one of them.

God could have said, "I'm good and the devil is bad." He did not say that. He said, "I am for you. Now, you be for me."

God could have said, "You are on the right track and your ex-friend is not. Don't bother with her. Stick with me and turn away from her." But He didn't. He said, "Come closer. Clear your body and your mind. Renew your faith. Come closer."

God could have said, "Well, you're doing fairly well. However, you need a little work over here on trust and a touch-up over there on fear." But He didn't. He said, "Surrender to me. Drop it all. Do not evaluate. Do not judge. Surrender."

God could have said, "Join up with me and I'll help you defeat the bad guys." But He didn't. He said, "If you turn to me, there is no bad. When you are with me, your fears disappear. Together we do not conquer, for there is no need. We live."

God could have said, "Don't listen to them. Listen to me." But He didn't. He said, "Your true ears are tuned only to me. Your false ears hear sounds that do not exist. Do not fear sounds that do not exist."

God could have said, "That devil is a mean old guy and he will get you if you don't watch out." But He didn't. He said, "Let yourself be forged on my anvil. Your pain is not to be feared. It is not real. It is only your becoming."

God could have said, "There is good and there is bad. There is me and there is the devil. There is love and there is hate. It is always one or the other. Black or white, right or wrong, this or that." But He didn't. He said, "Kneel before me. Love me. Trust me. Come."

God could have said, "Hate the devil. Fear him. Loathe him." But He didn't. He said, "Surrender."

***   ***   ***   ***   ***   ***   ***

God had given me a marvelously concrete way to practice surrender and trust. Every time I went to a grocery store I deliberately walked past the beer shelves just to feel the peacefulness that enveloped me as I passed by empty-handed. I walked past the shelves of wine offering delighted prayers of thanks to God. I managed to refrain from falling on my knees and shouting hallelujahs in the middle of the A&P, but my prayers filled its aisles on many days.

I struggled for a week, only a week, with the harsh words and accusations that had been dealt to me by my friend. One week was record-breaking time for struggling with a major dilemma. My alcohol-free mind was clear and my commitment was strong. Nevertheless, there were several questions that continued to distress me. How could I reconcile that what for me is a path to God is for another person demonic? How does it make sense that the experiences that turn me more and more strongly towards the heavens bring another person pain and anguish? How does that make any sense? How can what is spiritually right for me be so wrong for another person?

I fought diligently against the temptations of self-righteousness and its deceptively comfortable answers. I thought, "It is her limited understanding and her lack of philosophical sophistication that cause her inability to see the truth in what I am experiencing and saying." That belief was very seductive and held a grain of something vaguely resembling truth. But once I looked at it under a magnifying glass I could see it was merely a fancy version of, "I'm good and she's bad; I'm smart and she's dumb; I'm right and she's wrong." I knew that those types of beliefs were irrelevant at best and spiritually destructive at worst. I also knew that indulging in the cheap thrills they offered was very risky. I successfully resisted them.

It was a little easier for me to resist the urge to play demonic tit-for-tat since devil logic had never appealed to me anyway.

However, I did hear occasional rumblings in my mind that made noises like, "It's the devil making her say that the devil made me do it."

I identified and resisted sociological explain-ism: "It's the vast differences in our socio-cultural and educational backgrounds that result in blah blah blah." I caught myself indulging in psychodiagnostic name calling and quickly shut down that show: "She is projecting her repressed fear and rage onto me and, furthermore, is exhibiting a very hysterical behavior pattern in response to blah blah blah."

For a week I carefully navigated my way through the mine field of defensiveness, self-righteousness, rigidity, counterattack, and assorted other soul-less diversions. I did not fall into the potholes that beckoned to me. This lesson was far too important to resolve with simple-minded cop-outs. It was very clear that no short cuts were allowed in this lesson.

My meditations were shallow during the week. My energies were totally given to maneuvering my way around the potholes and pitfalls. My eyes stayed close to the ground.

Finally, by the end of the week I was ready for some answers, and Guardian Angel came to me during a meditation. He assured me that I had done my fair share of the work, and now he would explain the unexplained, clarify the muddled, and shine light into the dark.

"The times of trust and faith are the anvil on which is forged the strength of the soul," he said. "When you learn trust or faith, what you learn is reality. It is the reality you have glimpsed in the past few days.

"There is one reality—that is God. In the universe as you know it there are no other realities. All else in your eyes, in your understanding, is allusion."

Osirin had spoken to me earlier about allusions. I felt compelled, however, to look up the word again, this time in my new dictionary (American Heritage Dictionary; Houghton Mifflin). An allusion is an indirect, but pointed or meaningful, reference. An allusion is different from an illusion in that an illusion is taken to be reality; it is an erroneous perception of reality. Illusion implies being deceived by perception or belief.

Allusion, on the other hand, *refers*. It refers to something other than what is seen.

"Remember," Guardian Angel continued, "only God is real. *All else is allusion*. Absolutely all else.

"Good allusions point to God. Bad allusions do not necessarily point away from God, but they muddy already unclear waters, they cloud already hazy eyes, and they confuse already ignorant minds.

"Your search in these days of trials of faith is not for truth since you already know TRUTH: God is the One and Only One Truth. There is no truth to search for. What you search for is the purest of allusions, the most accurate of pointers to God, the clearest of teachings as to what is true.

"If you know the Truth—God—then you may choose your preference as to what is true. This means that you may choose your path. Many things, many pointers, many teachings are true. But none of them contains Truth. That is the key. Nothing that you see, think, or study on your plane contains the Truth. It hardly matters whether you follow course A or B or C if you do not know the Truth, for none of them will give you Truth. If you do know the Truth—God—then any course will provide pointers, beams of light that shine powerfully in the direction of God.

"Now, more about faith. Faith teaches you to abandon fear and doubt. Faith teaches you to ignore allusions when necessary and to focus on the only reality that exists—God.

"It is relatively easy to focus on God when there is no opposition, no fear, no panic, no threat, no danger. You are human. Your instinct is, and shall remain, to escape from fearful situations. Yet in this school you must learn that what you fear is allusion at best and illusion at worst. To abandon what is real—God—out of fear of what is not real is to fail the test of faith."

"Guardian Angel, may I interrupt?" I asked.

"Yes," he answered.

"So you are saying that my friend's accusations about the devil are simply her allusion—one of the signposts along her path to God?"

"Yes."

"And you are saying that if her allusions point her toward God, then they are true for her. And if my allusions point me toward God, then they are true for me. And yet, no allusions are Truth—they simply point and direct one toward Truth. Right?"

"Yes," he said.

"So, what she said to me has nothing to do with the devil. It has to do with the conflict between allusions."

"Yes. You have been told before about evil. This lesson has nothing to do with evil. It has to do with faith. You decide through faith whether to be willingly forged on the anvil. Yes or no. You struggled this week with faith. You considered no as your answer."

"I made a mistake, Guardian Angel. I took my allusions too seriously. I allowed her allusion to threaten my allusion as though my allusion itself were Truth. I imagined that her allusion was at war with my allusion, that one had to be right and the other wrong."

"What points you towards God is sacred for you," Guardian Angel said. "Abandon God for no one. Abandon your allusions for no one, or you risk the despair that darkens the soul's light. Alter your allusions only when clearer, brighter ones enter your heart as teachers of Truth."

"Thank you, Guardian Angel. Thank you from my heart."

"Now, others have asked you about Jesus," Guardian Angel continued. "And you ask us."

"Yes. My Christian friends are having trouble with where Jesus fits into my journey. It hasn't seemed like a problem or a burning question to me, but it is to them."

"I speak to you on your path," Guardian Angel cautioned, "not to them on theirs. I will give you your answer. They have their answer. Every answer is an allusion, theirs being as right as yours.

"This is what is True: Jesus and God are one. You know that. From that point on, all is allusion.

"Jesus is God in man. It is as though Jesus is the God essence within the human soul. In that sense you cannot reach God without Jesus, for you surely cannot reach God by turning away from your own soul. Jesus is the pure, total form of God incarnate. You are a much lesser form of the same—of Jesus-ness.

"Jesus came as a totally incarnated God-being in order to teach the Truth, which He did. And the Truth is always the same. God is Truth and the human soul is a bit of God.

"Remember—to the extent that you are your soul, you are at one with God and Jesus. The energy is all the same. There are no boundaries when God energy flows. It is like a river, many bits and particles flowing inseparably as one toward the same source.

"Jesus is your guide and your example. When He lived on earth He was His God self.

"That you stay away from the dogma of the church is your choice. It is neither right nor wrong. Do not be either proud or doubtful of your choice. Jesus is real. The church is an allu-sion. If the church points to God, it is a good allusion. If it points away, it is a poor allusion.

"One more thing—there is no truth as you think of truth. None. Your truths are all metaphors, as-thoughs. They are al-lusions. You cannot exist on your plane without allusions. So use them. And choose them wisely. Good allusions lead to Truth. Good allusions lead to God."

CHAPTER ELEVEN:

THE NEW FRIEND

The books I chose to read during the next phase of my journey were all on spiritual subjects. I read no psychology books, no gardening or horticulture texts, no books on nursery management, no novels of relaxation and escape. I filled my hours consuming all sorts of works on spiritual matters. I read books about Christianity, Judaism, Hinduism, Buddhism, Taoism, and several other -ism's. I read Western teachers speaking on religions of the East. I read Eastern teachers explaining the beliefs of the West. My appetite was insatiable, and truth in every flavor tasted delicious.

East and West began to blend. I stumbled upon the same lessons over and over again no matter whether I was reading Patanjali, Buddha, Lao Tsu, Ram Dass, Genesis, or the Gospel According to Luke. Truths repeated themselves. Truth seemed like a Häagen-Das store—many flavors, all delicious, and all of them the same thing.

There was one lesson that repeatedly caught my attention. In order to find God, say sages of East and West, one must go beyond the imprisoning limits of one's mind or one's ego. To find God, some part of the self must die and another must be born.

I began to feel very comfortable with that idea. I became so comfortable with it and so glib with it as a philosophy of life that I could rattle off the lesson in many different languages. I could say, "Be here now." I could say, "Strive for your Christ-consciousness, for the inner Kingdom of God," or "Learn yogic control over inner thought waves in order to recognize the Atman," or "Become a Bodhisattva—become the nothingness." I could say, "Balance is the key; live the Tao," or "Be a right-minded teacher of God; live in God's miracles." In shorthand I could say, "Drop the ego."

I was multi-lingual in telling myself that I must learn to gain mastery of my mind and my ego. I could give myself this advice in so many different languages that I was quite surprised to recognize one day that I didn't have the vaguest idea what I was talking about.

"Osirin, help!" I called out with my characteristic desperation. "I am trying diligently to drop my mind and my ego, and I just realized a very unsettling fact. I don't know what a mind or an ego is! I'm so embarrassed; I have been a psychologist for ten years and I don't know what an ego is. Osirin, I'm going to have one hell of a time throwing out the garbage if I can't even tell what, who, or where the garbage is."

"Well said, little one," replied my celestial guru. "So, relax. I have said before that your mind itself is not the problem. Now is the time to understand my words. You must observe. Listen, watch, and observe your mind. That is all. Do that now."

"Observe my mind? OK. My mind—let's see. I'm watching my mind. First of all, it lives inside the boney encasement known as my head. It is my thinker. It is my brain. No, wait. It is not my brain. My brain is something different. My mind . . . my mind . . . my mind is what produces my thoughts. Or maybe my mind *is* my thoughts. No, thoughts are energy waves produced by the brain. Or are they produced by the mind? What is the difference between my brain and my mind? And what are thoughts? And what on earth is my ego? Oh, no. Now I'm totally confused!"

"Little one, relax! Don't think. Relax. Meditate."

I began to meditate. Many times I would find myself focused on a lovely image, an unfolding lesson. Suddenly my mind would intrude with its random thoughts, fragmented images, and meaningless chatter, all of which accomplished absolutely nothing other than to distract me from what was important. I carefully observed my mind throughout that meditation and I wrote:

"My mind is still, calm. I allow whatever enters awareness to come. I see soft clouds. I relax. I try to send loving energy toward God. My mind jumps away from thoughts of God to thoughts of chicken cacciatore. I have not eaten chicken cacciatore for over ten years, but it seems to hold precedence in my mind at this moment over God. Now chicken fades and memories of telephone numbers that I memorized as a child return. My grandmother's telephone number was 45357. My home number was 45405. Slow, mind. Stop. Quiet. Release the noise. Calm the jibberish. Focus on breathing. Inhale. Slowly. Exhale. Feel the calm return.

"Images of Jesus enter my mind. Where did He come from? He sits on a simple throne. I approach Him from His left side. Entering into His energy feels like walking into a waterless shower of warmth. I feel Him all around me. If only I could have walked in His presence while He lived on this earth—if only I could have been in His physical presence, then maybe I would understand Him better.

"My mind is quiet. Very still. No thoughts. I sit quietly by the left side of Jesus' throne.

"It is hard to stay here mindlessly. I hear the rain on the roof. How many inches of rain is this? What a terrible drought we have had. When was the last time I watered the garden? Quiet, mind, quiet. Let it go. Return to Jesus.

"Jesus is no longer there. I see my mind running wildly like a child on a playground, interested only in its own pleasure. My mind runs with reckless and undisciplined abandon. I call to my mind, asking it to come back, to join in a greater quest. It does not heed my call. It is like a child, stopping to examine whatever passes in front of it. First a butterfly, then a blade of grass, then a piece of dirt, then a rock. My mind does not seek truth; it seeks stimulation and experience. It seeks whatever passes through it.

" 'There is more, mind. There is more than this! Join me.' My mind continues to run. I end my meditation for the day."

*** *** *** *** *** *** ***

A few days later I wrote: "I am in a lull. A dull lull. I am calm but confused. No desperation clouds my search today, but I do not feel peace. I feel empty. Each time I meditate I see my mind whirring in its meaningless mode. In the past I did not notice so much. My mind would whirr away, speaking jibberish and nonsense, and I would hardly notice. Jibberish inside my mind has been the norm for several decades. It is hardly extraordinary, but now I notice. Now jibberish annoys me. If I can't hear God or Osirin in my mind, I will settle for simple words of wisdom. If I can't hear wisdom, peace and quiet will suffice quite nicely. But jibberish? Spare me, my mind. Spare me the jibberish."

***　***　***　***　***　***　***

I was sitting in meditation a week later, still perplexed by how to rid myself of the noise between my ears. During that meditation I wrote: "The nonsensical meanderings of my mind through its labyrinth of jibberish are irritating me greatly. My mind resists my efforts to keep it harnessed, channeled, or focused. When my mind runs free, it never runs to anything of meaning. It always runs to its inner files of worthless nonsense. Yet, when my mind is harnessed, when it is settled into meditation, if I let go the reins just slightly, then my mind soars into new dimensions. Images come which are profound teachers. Words come to me from my guides and heavenly gurus. Awareness clarifies and wisdom unfolds.

"There is such a frustratingly fine line between wisdom and nonsense.

"I wish I could fine tune my skills at the controls of my mind. I imagine my mind as a Lear jet. My soul is the pilot and my ego is the co-pilot. When my ego is off duty or pleasantly cooperative, the Lear jet soars with ease through the skies to new adventures and new destinations. When my ego is uncooperative or unaware and takes over the controls, the jet flies aimlessly through the skies with no direction, no sense of purpose, sometimes barely avoiding collisions with trees and mountaintops.

"I begin to see more clearly that my mind is not the enemy. My mind is my Lear jet. My mind is my vehicle, or at least one of my vehicles. I must practice thanking my mind instead of condemning it. I must practice appreciating my mind. It is not the jet's fault for flying to absurd destinations when, in fact, it is the pilot who is misdirected and misguided."

Osirin appeared quite unexpectedly saying, "Good, little one! Good. Now, I will write to you of your thoughts. They are like bits of dust flying through the inner spaces of your being. Your thoughts are the creative tools of your soul. If you focus on thoughts of no consequence, then you create meaninglessness. If you focus on thoughts of destruction, then you create that which destroys. If you focus on thoughts of glory, then you create glory. It is as simple as that.

"Your mind must become your servant, not your master. Your mind can help lead you to God. But remember, a mind which is not harnessed and directed by the soul has the power to destroy.

"Do not see your mind as your enemy. It, too, is a valuable tool, an essential vehicle in your journey to God. Harnessed, it will carry you gracefully to God's door. Unharnessed, it will destroy you."

***   ***   ***   ***   ***   ***   ***

The next day I struggled in meditation for over an hour to harness my mind as Osirin had instructed. Finally in frustration I said to my disincarnate professor, "This is very hard, Osirin. I feel despair. I cannot hear the difference between my mind and your words. What is it I am supposed to be learning? Oh, yes, I'm supposed to be learning that my mind is not the enemy. Either it serves my soul or it does not. But how do I use my mind in the service of my soul? How do I train my mind?

"My mind and my ego are not the same. But what is the difference? I don't understand today, Osirin. What is it I am trying to be rid of? And how? How do I do it?

"This pressure in my head doesn't feel good today. It won't move. It won't open. It just sits there hurting. No answers are coming. My headache is building.

"I give up. Oh, Osirin, I don't mean I-GIVE-UP. I'll *never* do that again! I just mean I'll try again tomorrow. I think I'll go do something really mundane. Maybe I'll even cook some chicken cacciatore."

***   ***   ***   ***   ***   ***   ***

The next day in meditation I immediately felt calm. My thoughts lifted effortlessly. Very soon after closing my eyes I could feel the shift from holding onto my thoughts to setting them free. I lifted smoothly out of my busy-ness. I began to feel below me the concerns of the day and above me the awareness that those concerns do not matter. The air above me felt clear, bright, and empty. Obligations, worries, and projects all melted away. When I lift into the peaceful realms, I am free. And in my freedom there is one and only one thing to do—to turn toward silence. God lives in the silence.

After a few minutes of silence, Osirin spoke. "Listen to your mind as it runs wildly through its infinite expanse of sky. It races past one thought, then another, then another, yet never stops long enough to explore or to find the truth. It is as though a missile blasted into space with no direction, no goal. It would go fast and far, but what would be learned? Let your mind be a rocket, well trained and rightly controlled. And let it blast inwardly, into your inner heavens. Do that now."

I allowed the image that Osirin suggested to form in my mind. I began to see myself sitting in the cone of a rocket ship. I saw myself as the co-pilot. My soul, Ophelia, was the pilot. As we began our flight, it seemed that we could travel inwardly only a very short distance before we hit the limits of my skin.

Osirin reminded me, "There are no limits. Release."

I released the idea of limits. Darkness was around us and enveloped the rocket. Soon light entered and became increasingly brighter. I looked out and saw signs of nothing other than empty space.

"Your inner being is as vast as the skies themselves, little one. Your inner being is God. Soar farther. Farther!"

"It is hard to let go of the sense of body," I said, "the sense that I can soar inwardly only to the limits of my skin. It is difficult to feel that the inner me is not limited by its casing. It is hard to feel that I am in a body and yet I am infinitely beyond my body at the same time."

"You are not, in truth, in that rocket ship traveling into the infinite forever. You *are* the infinite forever. You are one with it," Osirin said.

"I can't feel that yet, Osirin. I can't feel it. I'm still in the rocket ship traveling away from home base, moving farther and farther away from a sense of body and earth."

"Then relax more. Do not let your mind run to seemingly more important issues."

"You caught me, Osirin. My thoughts just reminded me that I have three hours to meditate and write. Osirin, these are three precious hours carved with care out of a very busy week. I don't want to waste my three hours on rocket ship imagery."

"Then fill your mind with the trivia of important thoughts. Do it now. Write empty profundities. Write insignificant meanderings into useless expositions of religion and philosophy. Write a few trite poems, too."

"I feel a little nauseous," I said, humbled by Osirin's upbraiding. "What disgusting invitations. I'll stay in my rocket ship."

I saw myself travelling very far from earth. Whatever bound me to earth seemed to dissolve. I could strongly feel that my mind was the rocket. If I stopped to question or wonder, the rocket would weave and wobble in space, slowing down and losing its direction.

Pressure built in my chest. I felt as though my heart was being massaged from deep within, as though someone was pushing outward from deep inside my heart. I heard a voice saying, "I go to prepare a place for you in my father's house."

I began to see brilliant whiteness around me. A person in white approached with his hands outstretched. He was beautifully graceful and radiated light all around him. "You are so beautiful," I said to him. "Who are you?"

He came closer and reached out to me. I recognized the scars in his outstretched hands.

"Welcome," I said gently. "Welcome."

*** *** *** *** *** *** ***

And so I met Jesus. I was surprised that He had appeared several times in my meditations and now held out His arms in loving welcome. In fact, I was very surprised. After all, I still have many axes to grind with the church that bears His name. Furthermore, the Jesus who had been taught to me during my childhood was hardly a being, it seemed, who would join hands with someone traveling such a radical and unorthodox path as I.

So it seemed. Nevertheless, Jesus became a regular visitor in my quiet moments and in my meditations. He appeared often, usually unbeseeched and unannounced. At first I felt quite shy about speaking to Him. I had become very comfortable talking with angels and other dead people, but talking to Jesus felt oddly like placing a personal call to the President on his private phone. It felt highly presumptuous.

I had been taught as a child to pray, and I prayed dutifully in those days. Praying never felt presumptuous then. But what I felt in my meditations was unrelated to what I had been taught as prayer. What I felt in meditation was akin to an intimate conversation with a dearly beloved friend. It was like lessons with the master.

I was reluctant to accept the permission that He offered. I was shy and dubious, as always, but He was persistent in His gentle appearances in my mind.

"Jesus, this feels almost embarrassing," I said to Him. "Here You are holding out Your arms to me. But, remember, Jesus, I was not so very nice to You for a lot of years. I completely turned my back on You. I said some pretty trashy things about You and felt very condescending toward people who spoke highly of You. Are You sure You haven't got me confused with somebody else? Are You sure this invitation is for me?"

Jesus smiled.

"And look, Jesus, there are lots of people down here who would think my talking to You like this is in very poor taste. I haven't attended a Sunday morning church service in so many years that I have completely lost count of how many years it has been. And I have to warn You, I don't have any intention of attending any either. Unless, of course, You ask me to."

Jesus nodded.

"And when you think about what constitutes being a Christian, most people would vote me out of the club in a flash.

I'm not sure this is proper, me talking to You. But, Jesus, I'm really growing to like Your presence in my life. I think I'm growing to love You."

"And so it shall be," He said.

As happens often when I'm in His presence, I felt that I was being filled up with fuel that shines brightly yellow and infuses every cell of my body with the joy of aliveness. That yellow fuel is the stuff I have grown to think of as Love.

Pressure built in my chest. The feeling found its way to my mouth and words of praise blurted out.

"You are incredible, Jesus! You are so utterly incredible. I guess You already know that, but I feel like telling You anyway. You are amazing, precious, radiant, tender ... you are incredible!"

Jesus stared into my eyes with a brilliance that penetrated my forehead. "Your awareness of me is your gift both to God and from God. Let it grow."

"Jesus, why have You come to me?"

"Because you invited me."

"How did I invite You? I have been reading about You lately. I have been studying You. Is that it?"

"No," He said.

"How then?" I asked.

"By opening your heart to me on Good Friday. Do you remember?"

"Oh, yes! I do remember. That feeling came to me unexpectedly as I was taking a walk. As I remember it, I thanked You for Your death. And, for the first time in my life, Your death and resurrection made sense to me. I remember feeling very sorry that few people were there to hold Your dead body. I remembered my Dad's dying and wished I could have held You and caressed Your dead body as I did his. I wished I could have offered You my tomb. In fact, I did offer. I offered You a place in my home. I had forgotten, but I remember now. Was that it?"

"Yes. You offered. I accepted."

I began to pray to Jesus as though that is what was expected of me. "Lord Jesus, grant me the wisdom and patience to hear Your words and receive Your guidance."

Osirin appeared unexpectedly and said with a cosmic grin,

"You were doing fine on wisdom and patience until you started praying."

I was startled until I understood his meaning. I laughed. "Forgive me. It's an old habit. I'm surprised it is still around."

"Doxologies are fine, but only when they burst from your heart," Osirin said.

"How should I pray to Him?"

"Through surrender. Through trust. Through journeys into His realm."

"My mind runs away from You, Jesus. My mind runs away from You even into heartless prayer. I'll keep returning until the day comes that I will live in Your presence all the time. It's time for me to go now into the other world. Stay close to me, Jesus, if You can and if You will. Stay close even as my jibberish-prone mind forgets all about You. Stay close."

***   ***   ***   ***   ***   ***   ***

The peace that I felt with Him was the peace I sense when I see a newborn baby resting with a full tummy on its mother's chest. It is a peace which knows no fear, no mindfulness, no ego, no personality, no needs, no worship, no adoration, no questions, no hunger, no thoughts, no memories, no past, no future. It is the peace of nothingness.

I had never felt that peace before.

***   ***   ***   ***   ***   ***   ***

Becca: Am I a Christian, Jesus?

Jesus: Ask that from your heart.

Becca: Oh, I see. My head asked that question. In my heart, I don't care whether I am a Christian or not. In my heart, I love You.

Jesus: That is your answer.

***   ***   ***   ***   ***   ***   ***

Becca: Wow, Jesus! I've been reading more and more about You. I can't seem to get enough. Do you have any idea how smart You are? Oh, yes, of course You do. What I wouldn't give to have lived in Your days, to sit on the ground at Your feet and listen to You teach.

Jesus: Sit at my feet today.

Becca: Yes. I do. I will. Teach me, Jesus. Teach me, teach me.

Jesus: Your quest for me is dangerous in the earthly sense. You will be asked much.

Becca: There is nothing else for me to do, Jesus. I remember Osirin's words, "There is nothing else to be. Nothing else."

Jesus: If you follow me in this day, it is no different from the days when I walked the earth. The requirements are great.

Becca: Where can I sign?

Jesus: Here.

(He points to my heart. In my mind I see a small temple. It looks like a very small Greek temple. I enter slowly. There is a large piece of parchment paper on a marble table. Beside the paper is a quill pen and a pot of ink. I pause after taking the pen.)

Becca: Jesus, I do this not knowing what You will ask of me. I know it sounds a little trite and melodramatic, but I'd rather die for You than muddle through this existence without You. I can't do otherwise. I can't resist Your invitation. I have nothing to lose. I laugh, Jesus. I have nothing to lose except money, two businesses, a family, a house, security, social prestige, physical comforts, and all the other things that middle class Americans work for. I have nothing to lose but those things. And there is nothing else to do. I sign.

CHAPTER TWELVE:

THE ILLUSION OF ONENESS

My mind continued to soar through turbulent times. It would often fly like a single engine plane through hurricane winds and rains, being thrown, tossed, and battered by the irrelevancies that filled it. Oh, for peace and quiet between my ears! How I longed for peace and quiet.

I read of a meditation technique that helped. I would imagine my thoughts as being cars on a busy highway. I imagined my thoughts as the cars, peace and quiet as the space between the cars. As the cars sped by I focused not on the cars themselves, but on the empty spaces between them. No matter how many cars zoomed by, I focused only on the emptiness. As I focused, the empty spaces began to stretch out. They became longer and deeper. Eventually the traffic would stop. Perhaps it was only for a few seconds, but eventually all stopped.

"Why, Osirin?" I asked. "Why do our minds work like flypaper? Why are our minds like Japanese beetle traps, luring disgusting little critters into their inner sanctums? Why?"

"Because you have forgotten your soul," he answered. "Any overworked muscle gets bulky and inflexible. Any overstuffed piece of furniture becomes awkward and uncomfortable.

"I must tell you over and over, little one, your mind is not the enemy. It is your blindness, your sleepiness, your narcolepsy that is the problem. You *want* to fall asleep. Over and over you want to fall asleep.

"An awake mind is not a collector of garbage. An awake

mind is like a crystal. It reflects what comes near. It sees what is near. It does not seek what is not near. It does not fabricate. It does not resist the quiet.

"You are not asked to throw out your mind. You are asked to strip it of unnecessary clutter. Continue cleansing it. The day will come when your house is finally clear.

"And ego—that is simple. The ego is the collection of protective mechanisms that claim to protect you from external threat. What these mechanisms defend against is illusion and what they protect you from is God's reality.

"Your soul needs no protection that is not already in her essence. Your ego protects nothing other than itself. Hear me clearly. Your ego protects nothing other than itself. It protects illusions—illusions of who you are and what the world should be. Defending your ego is like protecting an empty field. There is nothing there of value to protect. In truth, there is nothing there at all to protect. The ego is an illusion claiming to be reality, and it defends itself as though it were reality. Your soul sits by, watching this ridiculous escapade, hoping that you will notice the absurdity and turn your attention away from nonsense. Your soul sits and waits."

"If it is so absurd, Osirin, why does everybody do it?"

"Because all of mankind must fight the same battle, overcome the same enemy, and learn the same lesson."

"What is that?" I asked.

"You know it already, little one:

   That you are not your body . . .

   That you are not your ego . . .

   That you are, by divine birthright, the child of God."

"Why is it so hard for us to know that, Osirin?"

"Because you are human. It is truly that simple, little one. The mystery of why it is so is not important now. What is important is that you must release what you are not in order to become what you are."

"I'm starting to see," I said. "It's death and re-birth, right?"

"Yes. Death and the first birth," he said.

"The *real* birth.
The reunion.
The re-union.
The atonement.
The at-one-ment.
The at-one.
The sacred Oneness."

***   ***   ***   ***   ***   ***   ***

Oneness—what a magical concept! I did not yet know its meaning, but, true to my character, I vowed to strive for it nonetheless. In my quest for oneness, I intensified my search for ways to drop my ego. For weeks I searched in vain for ways to rip it away like one might rip off a Halloween mask. At times I felt like a novice surgeon opening up a body and not being able to tell a diseased appendix from a healthy liver. Nevertheless, I persisted in my passionate quest for egolessness and oneness.

Some marvelous new discovery, a miracle of Godly proportion, felt as though it were hiding around the next corner. I excitedly awaited the arrival of this miracle, and in my untutored excitement, assumed that my personal taste of Cosmic Oneness were imminent.

In my eagerness I unwittingly concocted several experiences that made me feel as though I were on the verge of enlightenment. In meditation one day my body felt trembly and cool, all of my energy felt as if it were lifting into my head, and my throat pulsed vibrantly. I felt as if I were being lifted out of or into something most magnificent.

The same thing happened the next day during meditation. I focused intently on the new sensation, wishing myself higher and higher. I began to feel as though I were part of the air around me, part of the floor beneath me, and part of everything in the room. "This is it!" I thought. "Oneness is descending on me, or I'm descending on it, or something. Wow!"

All of a sudden I felt a hand descend from above me. It felt as though it were pushing me down. It pushed me into my body, into the solidity of the floor. Osirin's voice said sternly, "This is not it."

I began to sink, physically and emotionally. Sadness filled me for hours, and I felt bleak and disappointed.

Becca: Osirin, I was on the verge of making it. I was so close! Now here I am feeling discouraged and despondent again. What is the deal?

Osirin: The deal is ego, little one. Ego.

Becca: But, Osirin, the oneness that I was feeling—the light, the lightness, the sense of being a part of what was around me, and all of that. How can you call that ego?

Osirin: Because it is.

Becca: No! It is *not* ego.

Osirin: Yes. Ego.

Becca: No, no! I won't believe it. I felt such beautiful feelings. I was so close to the feeling of oneness. I felt lifted. I felt nearly transformed. I was so close!

Osirin: And what else was your I-I-I doing during those moments of near enlightenment?

Becca (sinking fast): Ohhhh. Oh, no. Ego.

Osirin: How could you taste of true oneness and still be saying I-I-I? You tasted the sweet syrup of the ego's best effort at fake oneness. Your ego concocted its very best imitation, its finest counterfeit. So, be grateful. You have looked deeply into the eyes of imitation oneness. Welcome back, little one. Welcome back to planet earth. From here we can travel.

CHAPTER THIRTEEN:

ONE STEP CLOSER TO ONENESS

My meditations began to change during the following weeks. I had learned much earlier that Spirit frequently switches gears on me, forcing me to be flexible so that I don't carve deep ruts as I travel my path. I had grown to accept the periodic changes, but this newest one was initially saddening. As I meditated, the voices I had heard clearly for almost two years became less distinctly recognizable. I could no longer clearly tell which voice belonged to Osirin, which to Dad, which to God, which to Jesus, which to Guardian Angel. Their voices began to run together, turning into something of a heavenly mush. I could feel their presence and hear their words, but I lost the ability to tell whose voice was whose and which energy belonged to which of my celestial friends.

I asked Osirin, "Why are you not so clear? What is happening? Where have you gone?"

A voice from the heavenly melting pot answered, "I'm here."

"But who are you?" I asked. "I can't distinguish you clearly anymore."

The voice answered, "So meditate on that. And meditate on the oneness you seek to understand."

I had known since my journey began that all the voices I hear come somehow from God. When I found myself suddenly thrust into a course on Oneness 101, however, I began to suspect that all my heavenly buddies are not simply part of God's team, but that they are all somehow intimately interwoven. I began to sense that they are not linked as a faculty of noted professors all assigned to teach me, not interwoven by being members of the same club, not joined even as servants of God. I began to see that they are linked somehow, inexplicably, as one.

I struggled with my new awareness, trying hard to understand. After a few days I admitted defeat.

"OK, Dad, Osirin, God, Jesus, and Ophelia," I said. "Whoever you are and wherever you are, this is as far as I can go with this oneness stuff. Somehow all of you folks are separate and yet you are one. That's as far as I can go. I understand it about as well as I understand the theory of relativity. I know it is so. Beyond that, I understand zilch."

     ***   ***   ***   ***   ***   ***   ***

For several months I couldn't meditate while I ran because I had given myself a bum hip from too much shoveling in the garden. I couldn't meditate in a Buddha-like posture for very long because I had given myself a bum back from picking up heavy pots at the nursery. And if I meditated in a prone position I'd fall asleep within a very few minutes. My favorite way to meditate became taking long and brisk walks, particularly at sunset.

Usually when I walked I plugged my ears into loud and joyous gospel music. With those sounds to propel me through space, my body was wondrously energized and steep hills melted under my feet. I focused my mind as intensely as I could on the words of praise and celebration that my friends sang through my earphones, and I practiced beaming those words out of my body and into the skies. At moments when all of my energy was powerfully concentrated on singing hallelujahs into the heavens, I felt as though I were beaming love directly and instantly to the heart of God. After three miles of that, I'd had quite a cardio-spiritual workout!

One day, however, my new mystery voice told me to walk without music. I didn't like the idea, so I conveniently concluded that the voice was merely a senseless muttering from the cesspool that lives somewhere deep within the left hemisphere of my brain. With my Walkman in my pocket and my earphones on my ears, I set out.

I made it as far as my mailbox before the voice said again, "No music today."

"But my feet won't know what to do," I complained. "And I'll be bored! And you know what else will happen? I will just think for three miles. I'll get nothing out of this walk other than a little more exercise for my already overdeveloped left brain. And, worst of all, that last killer hill will be impossible to climb without music."

"No music."

"OK, OK, OK."

On that walk I did not send hallelujah love letters to God and I did not conquer the killer hill in record time. However, I did begin to understand something more about oneness. As I walked I thought of rivers. All rivers begin in basically the same way. They begin as springs welling up from the earth, they begin as channels that collect melting mountain snow, they begin as conduits of rain water. They all begin in basically the same way.

After a river begins its flow, it takes on a character of its own. The Nile is very different from the Mississippi, the Ganges different from the Seine. Each has its own character, its own personality. Yet they all flow in the same way toward the same destination.

I began to wonder what it is like when rivers flow into the ocean. I wondered if water particles from the Seine flow up to particles from the Nile and say, "Hi, I'm from the Seine. Where are you from?" I wondered if the rivers struggle to maintain their own identities within the ocean, the Ohio River careful to keep its separateness from the waters of Cripple Creek. I have never been privy to the conversations between rivers as they meet in the middle of the ocean, but I doubt that is what happens. I imagine the Mississippi River willingly surrenders its Mississippi-ness as it becomes ocean. I imagine it all somehow becomes one. Completely and totally one.

Rivers and oceans—all one. All the same. And yet somehow separate. There is part of the Nile that is now the ocean, and yet the Nile still exists as the Nile. The Nile is the Nile, the

Nile flows toward the ocean, and the Nile *is* the ocean, and all three statements are true at the same time.

Suddenly I could see that there are no contradictions, and I began to understand that I am Becca, I am Becca moving toward God, and I am God-ness. All at the same time. All at exactly the same time.

After checking to see if any earthly beings were near, I turned my face to the sky and spoke aloud: "OK, you Big Boys, I think I'm starting to get it. At those moments when I am no longer 'me' but am, instead, my soul—at those moments I am a drop of water in God's ocean. And in those precious moments I am somehow joined and united with all of you. I am not joined with you the way marriage or membership joins. I am *one* with you. I melt into you and you into me. I become a tiny particle in the ocean, and I am one with all other parts of that ocean.

"I say it and I believe it, but I still can't quite comprehend it. If it is true, then there is a part of me that is already in the ocean. There is a part of me that is already completely and totally one with God. There is a bit of me, somewhere deep inside, that is God-ness. It's getting clearer. It's starting to make an iota of sense. But only an iota."

***   ***   ***   ***   ***   ***   ***

I woke up the next morning very confused and virtually obsessed with the idea of oneness. In my morning meditation I wrote: "This oneness business feels very important, but overnight my IQ took a nose dive. Yesterday I almost understood a fraction of it. Today I understand nothing, absolutely nothing. I look at my body. I seem to end at my skin. I don't understand how it works. How can I be in this body and also be one with what is around me? It makes no sense."

I heard a voice in my head, a voice from the melting pot. The voice said, "Don't be dumb. You are not five years old and God is not a kindly old man sitting on a throne. Re-think God."

"No, no, no!" I insisted. "I want God to be tangible. I want God to be in a form I can understand. I want God to be like the pot of gold at the end of the rainbow. I want God to be sitting in a fancy diamond-studded throne at the end of my path!"

"That is a charming little illusion," said the voice.

"Don't make fun of me! I'm trying hard and you are supposed to teach me."

I tried to relax and resume my meditation. My frustration resisted my efforts to calm it. My irritability defied all attempts to breathe peacefulness into my body. I felt about as much lightness and lift as if I were riding in a hot air balloon filled with concrete blocks.

"I am calling a meeting," I defiantly announced into the sky. "I am sending an official invitation to any of you Big Boys who are willing to attend. I'm mad today—just plain mad. I feel irritable, mean, and extremely dumb. Consequently, I seem unable to levitate my energy into floaty mode, so I'll talk to you today from down-to-earth Western logic. This is the agenda for the meeting: *I want some answers!*

"Look, guys, there are plenty of people running around down here in bodies who think I am one-half to three-quarters nuts. They think I'm nuts because I talk to you. Long ago I gave up not talking to you because it's clear that if I turn my back on you I really will be nuts. Of course, they will think I'm sane again, but I'll be bonkers. So, I will not turn my back on you. However, I would like to know a few things, and I'd like to know them now. I'll get right to the punch line. What on earth is going on here and how does all of this work?"

"Interesting questions," said the mystery voice. "Could you be a bit more specific?"

"Specific? Sure, that's easy. Being specific is no problem at all for someone whose walls drip with diplomas granted by institutions of Western logic. Being specific, scientific, and intellectual is no problem at all. Question 1: Who is Osirin? Is he the same as the being I feel is Jesus? Question 2: Is the being I feel to be Jesus really Jesus? Question 3: Did Dad really appear to me the morning after he died or was that some other energy? Did I actually see his spirit or did I see, (a) a materialization of my own thoughts, (b) another spirit being, (c) an inanimate energy field of some kind, or (d) an old-fashioned, garden-variety hallucination? Question 4: Is Jesus and/or God really inside of me? How does that work? What does that mean? Is that literal or poetic? Question 5: When I write, who is it who writes to me? Is it Osirin? Is it Osirin writing through my personality, through my style? Is it just me alone tapping into some pool of creativity floating around in the skies? Is it my soul? Or is it me, just plain me all by myself? And now for the big question: What in God's name is one-ness?"

Osirin's energy approached clearly and recognizably. "Your questions are delightful," he said.

"Logic, Osirin. I want logic, not delight. By the way, wel-come back."

"Your insistence is delightful, little one."

"OK, Osirin. Ha, ha, ha. There's a little delight. Now, let's get to answers."

"Smile, little one. One real smile and then I can penetrate your barrier of mind, your walls that are so carefully con-structed of one IQ point cemented tightly to the next IQ point. Smile. Yes! Delight with me in your questions so I might have access to your heart, for only there will my answers make any sense or receive any welcome.

"Now that I see your lovely smile I can proceed. Be very still. Listen to the music. Give me the hand. Go slowly. Do not second-guess me. Do not predict my words. That's better. Let your mind soar with deliberate speed toward the skies, and I will speak as you soar.

"We are all one—you, your father, your angel, I, God, Jesus, your soul—all one. So, when you ask if it is one or the other, you miss the answer. When you ask if it was your father you saw, your mind poses the question in a way in which no answer is true. Your questions imply separateness and duality. When you ask from duality, there are no answers. There is no duality except in the mind which phrases these questions. When you write as now, you allow your oneness to be. You do not resist it or fight it. It makes no difference if you imagine that you speak to me—Osirin—or to God, or to a stone, or to a daffodil. Do you see? The true God, the living God, is ALL, and any that is one with God can and will be one with you if you allow oneness.

"You see that the oceans do not declare their separateness. No, it is the mind of man that separates, labels, and names the oceans. And your soul does not separate you from me, from your father, or from God. It is your mind that does that.

"It is hard, little one, hard to feel. Keep moving ahead. The day of clarity will come. There is no God on a throne. There is no God with a long beard. God is not bound by skin. God is not bound at all. God *is*. God is is-ness. God is the very meaning of is. God is life. God is each and every thing that is.

"Remember this—what you think of as God is but His shadow. You vaguely sense the shadow that is cast when light shines around Him. You have not yet sensed His essence. Slow and steady, little one. Slow down.

"You may feel a personal attachment to me for now. You may feel a personal attachment to Jesus for now. That is fine. That is very helpful, as this attachment teaches love, humility, patience, trust, and devotion. All are essential lessons on the path. But in truth there is no separateness between Jesus and God. There is no Jesus per se. There is God, and one of His most glorious manifestations is Jesus. There is no Becca per se. You, too, are a manifestation of God."

***　　***　　***　　***　　***　　***　　***

Osirin: Today the lesson will be on the subject of "Who am I?"

Becca: Good grief, Osirin. I thought I was beyond that lesson. That is routine, ordinary identity crisis stuff. I thought I was at least advanced enough to be having spiritual crises.

Osirin: Very cute. But I think you missed the point. Answer me, little one: Who are you?

Becca: Oh, Osirin. Must I?

Osirin: No, but I would highly recommend it.

Becca: OK. For starters, I'm Becca Zinn. And I'm thirty-seven years old. Oh, I'm starting to get your point. Becca Zinn and 37 are totally irrelevant. Right?

Osirin: Right. Go on.

Becca: Well, I'll try for more meaningful attributes. I am a psychologist and nurserywoman. Those are the ways I choose to perform my tasks and services in this world. Uh-oh, Osirin. That's not any better, is it?

Osirin: No. You're on track. More.

Becca: I'll try for the real stuff. I am a person who is questing for God.

Osirin: That's trite.

Becca (with wounded pride and injured feelings): Why?

Osirin: Look up trite, and go to number 2.

Becca: Trite, definition number 2, is frayed or worn by use. Under definition number 2, my dictionary says to see the root word ter in the appendix. Ter means to rub away, to remove outer coverings, as rubbing cereal grain to remove the husks and thence to the process of threshing either by the trampling of oxen or by flailing with flails. I get it! Osirin, you are a magician with words. Trite means overused and worn out. It contains within it the word rite, which is a religious ceremony. And its root refers to the process of transforming something by rubbing away the outer coating. Uh-oh, I had it, but now I've lost it. What does all that have to do with who I am?

Osirin: You tell me.

Becca: Oh, yes! I see. It always comes back to this, doesn't it, Osirin?

Osirin: And where else would you expect it all to lead?

Becca: The husks surrounding the grain are the Becca Zinn, the psychologist, the nurserywoman, the physical attributes, the personality, the ego, and, in short, absolutely everything that I think of as Becca Zinn.

Osirin: Bull's eye. Go on.

Becca: And the grain is . . . is . . . is . . . God.

Osirin: Right.

Becca: Osirin, this is sinking in. It's barely penetrating my dull mind, but it is sneaking through the gates as the guards sleep. Osirin, I am God. The real "I," not Becca Zinn, but the real "I"—I am God. Right?

Osirin: Yes, little one. You and I together. And all other souls. All.

Becca: A flood of awareness is pouring in, Osirin. Let me try to grasp these thoughts. I'll write them quickly and study them later. Duality is the only evil. Duality is the only sin. The way to God is through oneness. The dangers of personality and ego lie in their perpetuation of the illusion of duality.

There is only one God. There is absolutely no duality. There is no Jesus separate from God, no you separate from God, no me separate from God. All truly is One. And the One is God. There is no duality except that created by us, and the creation of that duality is our sin, our karma, and our pain. The only freedom is in oneness, and the only way to God is through the oneness that is and has always been within us.

Osirin: Welcome, little one. Take my hand. Even those thoughts—put them down. Join with me. Take my hand. Now be one. Journey with me into the One.

In previous journeys with Osirin I had travelled in rockets, flown with wings of an angel, walked on stars, floated on clouds, and danced on rainbows. This day, however, was different. Osirin took my hand and we began to walk. As we walked a strange thing happened. An energy who held hands with Osirin walked out of my body. She and Osirin moved forward while I remained still. As they moved farther away from me, I felt deeply sad and alone. I had to make a choice. The choice was simple. The choice was which me to be, the me in the body that I call Becca or the me who was walking with Osirin. I could not be both. As my emptiness intensified, the decision was clear. I wanted to be with Osirin. I projected my mind into the being who held his hand as strongly as I could, and I began to feel identified more and more clearly with her. I felt a snap, as though I became disconnected from the body and the personality that were now behind me. At that moment I was free. I had no body. Osirin and I were together, formless and floating. There were no words. No images came to my mind. My meditation was filled with love, energy, and light. And yet there was nothing ... nothing ... the Divine Nothing the Buddha speaks of. For a few short, glorious minutes I merged with my beloved Osirin, and I felt the majesty of God's infinite, awesome, radiant Nothing.

CHAPTER FOURTEEN:

JOURNEYS INTO THE EYES

"You have everything you need for your journey," said Osirin. "You are packed and ready to go. This is a journey into a very new land. This is a place known only to those who deeply wish to know it. It is unlike any place you have seen or any place you have known. When you arrive there you will be in your inner wilderness, in the inner place that is completely new, unknown, and uncharted to you. You will journey into the inner reaches of time. You will see miracles in their making. You will witness creation.

"You must choose. The risks are greater in opening your eyes now than in opening your eyes as you die. That is the peril. It is not safe to see before you die. You must choose. What do you wish to do?"

I heard a voice within me say, "I have pledged my troth."

"Who said that?" I wondered. "Who answered for me? And what does troth mean?"

I was told to look up the word and, for once, I was assigned to definition number 1. Troth, number 1, means good faith or fidelity.

I realized the voice was Ophelia's and it is she who knows quite well what troth means. It is she who never doubts Osirin, never falters when he leads, and never questions his oneness with God. When Osirin says, "Let's go," Ophelia says, "My troth is pledged."

Ophelia spoke to Osirin saying, "I never wished to be parted from you, and now I wish to return. I have no fear of the perils.

I have no need to remain apart from you, no wishes left to fulfill, no illusions left to explore. My wish is for the reunion, and I have educated Becca well enough that she will not interfere."

"That is so," I said. "I am ready."

***   ***   ***   ***   ***   ***   ***

I was packed for my journey and my troth was pledged. There was only one slight hitch in my travel plans. As usual, I had no idea where I was going. This time it was Jesus who appeared in my meditation with itinerary in hand.

Jesus said, "This is what is to be next. When the time presents itself for your further education in this sacred school, this shall be your path. You shall learn of forgiveness—forgiveness of yourself for all the gifts you have abused. Your awareness will bring you pain, and your pain will lead you to the door of genuine self-love."

As I ended my meditation I was grateful for the words I received from Jesus. I felt cleansed from the peaceful respite, but I did not understand the reference He made to the abuse of gifts. I searched my mind for clues, for evidence of abused gifts. At first I could not see a single example of blatant abuse. Then I recognized alcohol. Yes, that one I could see. I certainly had used alcohol as a means of avoidance and escape, as a tool in the service of blindness. Beyond that, however, my record looked fairly clean.

Later that evening as I talked with my husband about the events of the day, I mentioned to him my lesson on the abuse of gifts. As I was telling him of my inability to identify the abuses Jesus spoke of, I stopped speaking mid-sentence as though the generators that power my thoughts and my voice had suddenly shut down. I found myself staring into his eyes and feeling deep, profound sorrow. "Those eyes," I thought, "those eyes, that heart, that man, that love—those are the very gifts I have abused."

Voice of Doubt (racing quickly to the rescue of my ego): He deserved every bit of it!

Becca: I know. So did I. We both learned some very hard

lessons through the trials of marital misery and mistrust. But look at those eyes.

Voice of Doubt: You had to go through the pain together in order to find your answers. People can't just fall in love and live happily ever after.

Becca: I know, V.D., I know. And I value the lessons we've learned through our pain. But that's not the point. The point is that I abused love.

Voice of Doubt: Well, so did he!

Becca: That's not the point. I abused love.

Voice of Doubt: You tried during those years. You tried hard. But the time wasn't right, and you weren't ready, and he wasn't ready, and . . .

Becca: I can't hear you, V.D. It's odd; you keep repeating yourself and I can't hear you. All I can hear is his eyes. I'm sorry, eyes. I'm very sorry.

***   ***   ***   ***   ***   ***   ***

I lay outside under the full moon later that evening. My husband joined me. Together we reviewed the gifts in our lives that we had abused. My record was no longer deceptively clean. Rather, it was filled to overflowing. Together we examined our pasts, and between us we found not one relationship, not one role, not one gift that we had not somehow abused. Together we gazed at the moon and reviewed our ever-lengthening lists.

It was a beautiful summer night. The full moon, which is often blamed for frazzling peoples' emotions, functions as a calming teacher for me. It was comforting to have her glowing on me from above and to have Victor by my side as I held out my arms to welcome the awareness of the greatest of all abuses, the deadliest of my sins.

The awareness approached me as though it emerged out of a dense fog. At first I could perceive only its enormity. "This is the big one, Victor," I said. "I can't recognize it yet, but this is the big one."

In a few moments its identity was clear. My cardinal sin stood before me. "Victor," I said, "I am guilty of abusing the gift of life."

During the years of our marital pain there were days and months when I did not value my life. I never held a razor to my wrists or a bottle of Quaaludes to my mouth. Perhaps worse, I disregarded my life and refused to honor the lessons that lived within my pain. During the years of struggle, I had not practiced patience and trust, and I had not welcomed pain as a teacher. Over and over again I had given up on life. And in doing so I had fortified the walls of my hell.

***   ***   ***   ***   ***   ***   ***

Over the next few days I looked deeply into the eyes of my cardinal sin.

Becca: You seduced me, sin. You seduced me into believing that a few years of anguish would be reason enough to turn against life. You trapped me in depression, rage, despair, and prolonged pain.

The Cardinal Sin: Do not blame me. It was you who chose me.

Becca: What do you mean?

The Cardinal Sin: I do not ask for believers. I do not proselytize. I am merely that energy which denies life and love. And I, too, am part of the Tao.

Becca: Really? You did not come after me?

The Cardinal Sin: No. You embraced me.

Becca: I guess so, sin. Oh, yes—yes, I see. It was only at the end of your path of excruciating pain and total despair that I could fall into God's arms. Knowing me, I never would have made it without you. Now my job is to forgive myself for having needed you. I thank you, Sin, but I deeply hope I'll never need your lesson again.

***   ***   ***   ***   ***   ***   ***

The next day Jesus appeared again in my meditation saying, "I will tell you more of love. In order to remove the notion that love is a feeling, meditate on a white lily. At this point in your growth you are approaching the ability to love. Until now what you have called love is merely caring, compassion, attachment, politeness, and concern. Those are not wrong, but they will not teach you love. You must go beyond, into the lily. The lily is life. It is unfolding. It is creation. It is God."

"I do not understand," I said.

"Look—the flower. Meditate on it. Do not be confused. Meditate until you see that you are the flower. Then you shall love."

I continued my meditation, turning my attention to mental images of lilies. I sat quietly and peacefully for a few minutes until I felt the familiar tingles in my left hand that signalled the need to write. I picked up pen and paper, and these words flowed from my pen: "As I continued my search for the meaning of oneness I stumbled upon a long lost relic, a memory from my past. I discovered deep inside a drawer of old treasures a necklace I had worn as a child."

The energy within the writing was clearly Osirin's. I interrupted my meditative calm to exclaim to him, "What necklace? What on earth am I—or you—talking about?"

I felt myself gently pulled toward a chest of drawers in the room where I was meditating. I opened the bottom drawer and searched through some small boxes until my eyes fell upon a particular old treasure. As soon as I saw it, I was sure. This was it—the forgotten relic Osirin had written about. I had discovered a mustard seed necklace that, indeed, I had worn as a child.

After holding the necklace for a few quiet moments, I put it around my neck. As I did, I began to feel younger and younger. In my mind I saw myself, eleven years old, kneeling at the altar of my childhood church. The eleven-year-old Becca was filled with innocent faith. It was the year before her trust would be pummeled and her naive faith in God would meet its demise in the "real" world. It was the last year of her innocence. It was the year before the reign of the ego began.

The necklace that once rested near an eleven-year-old heart now rested at the tender spot at the base of my thirty-seven-year-old throat. My throat, which had been strangely sore for weeks, began to feel well, and I began to cry. I wept for the innocence I had lost.

The child at the altar knew nothing yet of sin, darkness, or evil. She was still clean, pure, and whole. She was a stranger to the abuses of the ego, the wickedness of misused free will, the destructiveness of blindness, and all the other poisons that had become so familiar to the adult Becca.

I could feel her innocent faith growing in me, sprouting like a mustard seed. "Where have you been, little girl? Where have you been?" I asked.

"Kneeling here for twenty-five years, waiting for you to return," she answered.

I took her in my arms at the altar and wept on her wise little shoulder. For the first time in my life I began to feel what it is like to love myself. For the first time I held the child of God who lives within me, weeping for the years of separation and for the reunion, and loving her. Simply loving her.

***　***　***　***　***　***　***

For weeks I had been practicing a meditation in which I would sit in front of a mirror, gaze into my own eyes, and try to see the "real me." I sensed that the meditation was very important, even though I was receiving no noticeable results. During those weeks I must have gazed at myself for ten hours or more, looking for something within or behind those eyes that would give me a clue of my true identity. I was looking for more contact with The-God-Within, but all I usually saw was a rather stoney face and semi-glazed eyes staring back at me.

The morning after I found the mustard seed, I was pulled to the mirror to repeat the into-the-eyes meditation. I cut a white lily from my garden and put it in a vase beside me. I plugged my ears into a recording of Bach's "Jesu, Joy of Man's Desiring," propped myself on the bathroom counter in a half-lotus position, and began to stare at myself. To any sane observer I would have looked like a complete nut.

My eyes fell to the mustard seed around the neck of the woman in the mirror. As I looked up at the face in the mirror I noticed that her eyes were filled with tears, and I felt deep compassion for her.

I began to wonder who "I" was and who "she" was. "Perhaps I am Ophelia," I thought, "and she is Becca. Or maybe I am my right brain and she is left brain, or vice versa. Or maybe I am the adult Becca and she is the eleven-year-old, or vice versa." The wonderings led only to meaningless confusion, so I quieted my mind and returned to her eyes.

The mirror seemed to disappear, and I felt that I was face to face with this being. She looked radiant. Love shone like moonbeams through the tears that filled her eyes. As a sensation of profound peacefulness swept over me, I gasped with deep relief and total surprise, "She loves me, too!"

I had totally forgotten that there was a physical mirror between us, so I was quite surprised when my hands hit a hard, cold surface as I reached out to embrace her. Being unable to hold her with my physical arms, I used my etheric, nonphysical arms instead, and we met heart-to-heart for perhaps the first time in my life.

"You are beautiful," I said to her. "I don't know why it has taken me so long to see you, to see your beauty. You are a child of God. You are a reflection of God, and you are beautiful just as you are. I love your expression of God. I even love that crazy, noisy mind of yours. I love your ego and your personality. I love everything you have been. I forgive you for all the mistakes you have made, and I release my anger at you for those things."

She began to weep. "I have waited so long for you. So long."

I responded, "I am very sorry. I spent many years of my life looking for love. I have looked everywhere except in your eyes. I spent many years looking for happiness and peace, and I have looked everywhere except to you. I have spent the two years since my father's death looking for God, and I have looked everywhere except in the mirror.

"I will love you for all that you are, and I will protect you from all you are not. I will no longer war against what you are. All that you are is a gift from God. All that you are is a miracle! And in treasuring what you are, I will war against what you are not. I will protect you from the abuses the world offers. I will shelter you from anything that might dim the light in your eyes. Most importantly, I will love you."

***　　***　　***　　***　　***　　***　　***

The next day Guardian Angel approached with a gentle warning.

Guardian Angel: You must be careful today.

Becca: I've been hearing you say that all day. Why do you keep telling me that?

Guardian Angel: You are reaching high. Very high. You are reaching higher than you have reached before. When you learn self-love you are beginning to reach very near to God's heart. And you must be careful.

Becca: Why? You make this sound so scarey. You seem to want to scare me away. You almost sound like Voice of Doubt.

Guardian Angel: I know this is so. But you know to trust me.

Becca: Yes, Guardian Angel.

Guardian Angel: You must be alert to the negative forces of Opening. When you open a long closed and sealed tomb, what emerges first is dust. Out will pour the air of deadness. You must be prepared for this or else you will be scared. You must fall back into the arms of love and safety.

Becca: I will.

Guardian Angel: Remember the image of the opening tomb. It will take a little bit of time to air out. The stench will dissipate in a short time, but you must allow it time.

Becca: Thank you. I will heed the warning. Is there anything I should do?

Guardian Angel: Return to the mirror in love several times a day. Endure the stench when it comes. Do not focus on it. Do not war against it. Allow yourself pleasures of the flesh in light moderation. Do not be stoic right now. Do not be indulgent either. Do not overstimulate any part of your mind or body. Be easy, very easy with yourself. And remember that light shines brightly behind grey clouds. Any clouds that appear are temporary, very temporary. But they may present themselves with more fury and more stench than you are prepared for.

Becca: Thank you.

Guardian Angel: A few days. That is all. A few days. Now, back to the mirror.

CHAPTER FIFTEEN:

ANOTHER BIRTHDAY

"I am Osirin," my hand wrote. "I write of important things today. I write of the next quest. It is the quest for the eternal wisdom that flows as your birthright in your veins. You seek what is yours. Even I, little one, even I cannot give it to you. Your beloved Jesus cannot give it to you. God gave you the gift when He breathed life into your being. The gift is given once, for once is all that is needed.

"Pray no more for the gift. Pray only for grace—the divine patience which God bestows on those who seek themselves. Pray no more for wisdom. Rather, pierce your veins and see what is within you.

"I speak to you of You, of the God-ness that You are. You must be You, the beloved of God, the holy One. For then You shall also be my reunited friend, my cherished and beloved little One."

    ***   ***   ***   ***   ***   ***   ***

"Remember the light bulb meditation, little one. You are a light bulb. God is the light. Today you are Becca—a body/mind/ego/personality. You are an unlit light bulb, a vessel designed to receive the light, but as yet dark and unlit. Tomorrow the power of God will rush into the bulb and fill it. And then Becca will be gone. When you stare at a lit light bulb, you do not see bulb-and-light. No. The bulb disappears and you see only light. When God truly moves into your bulb, into your Becca, then Becca will be no more. And that will be the day of your birth."

***　　***　　***　　***　　***　　***　　***

As I begin my meditation on this day, thoughts spin through the inner cinema screen of my mind with more determined gusto than usual. Images of grotesque creatures from last night's movie mingle with images left over from watching the Fourth of July fireworks in New York City. Fireworks, monsters, and busy-ness of the day all intermix to create an impossible mush.

I imagine ladling the gooey mush out of my mind with a 24-karat gold soup ladle. It seems to work.

Guardian Angel comes to me strongly and clearly. He brings the last message I am to receive from him for a very long time. He delivers to me a profound new responsibility and a gift of far-reaching hope.

Guardian Angel says, "I come to bear glad tidings of joyful news. A child is born. And he shall be the Prince of Love, the Prince of Peace. And his light shall be unto all who will receive it. His name is Peace, and the child is within you. The child is born to you, within you.

"You are the mother—and the child. You are the growing Christ child. Kneel before your child. Then wrap him in soft clothes and begin your journey.

"Love the child. Be his mother. Raise him to manhood. And then die to him, willing to him absolutely all that you have.

"Light a candle each day in his honor. And nurture the light that is your Christ child.

"I send you my love for the last time. You need me no more for now. The child is born."

***　　***　　***　　***　　***　　***　　***

As I lit the first candle, I bade a loving and accepting adieu to my beloved Guardian Angel. The reasons for his departure mattered little, and, trusting in my knowledge that abandonment is not possible in Spirit, I thanked him for his gifts and released him with love. To my father I sent a bouquet of my tears and deep gratitude for the most precious of all gifts, the one that launched me on my voyage two years earlier. I reached for Osirin with my left hand and for Ophelia with my right, and I said to them, "It is here that we begin. Together let us raise this child."

APPENDICES
AND
WORDS OF WISDOM

GUARDIAN ANGEL on POWER

Power is not force, yet power does have force within it. Power is not control, yet power often results in what appears to be control. Power is a life force, just like the lightning. Lightning occurs quickly. So does the thunder that follows in its wake. The traces that it leaves in the atmosphere are purifying. Sometimes it destroys something as it releases its power, yet that is the way of life. Destruction is not bad or evil, but the chaos of half-hearted lightning—that is bad. The destruction caused by such blockages, the blockage of half-hearted lightning, is far more potent than the potential danger of standing under the tallest tree in the field during an intense lightning storm.

Neither power nor lightning is tangible. Neither is in your possession. Each is potent energy which cleanses, clears, clarifies.

That fear of power in the pit of your stomach—that is the main block between yourself and your soul.

Be the lightning. Fear it not. Its power cleanses your universe. Its electricity is no different from the electricity of your soul. Do not be a half-hearted heart. Do not be a half-souled soul. Be the lightning.

OPHELIA on THE CHOICE

Here stands a lovely maiden. There stands a wretched creature, an ugly shrew. Choose. To be a lovely maiden requires only one thing—love. It is your choice.

OSIRIN on GOODBYE

Tides turn. All things on earth change. Nothing changes in heaven. The things that change on earth must be bid farewell with a kiss. To say goodbye is a blessing. Imagine if all things did remain and nothing could be shed. All sheds—which allows eternal newness. You must see newness. Newness is the mother of rebirth.

GUARDIAN ANGEL on THE WEAPON

You wonder why we speak so much of love. It is not that we are poets. We are warriors of God. Your earthly warriors fight with guns and swords. We do not have such weapons, nor would they do us any good if we had them. Our only weapon is love. It is more powerful than anything in the universe and is the only weapon we need. Whether as a weapon it is powerful enough depends greatly on you and your fellow man.

OSIRIN on ANGER

Your heart is corrupted still by the anger you have been feeling. It is a sign of negative forces at work in you. All negative forces must be cleansed. There is no justifiable reason for your anger. Prolonged anger is always a sign that your ego is captured by the enemy. If there is no ego to capture, anger is impossible. Remember that. There are no exceptions.

GUARDIAN ANGEL on JOY

There is a long way to travel between here and there. The steps are sometimes fast, sometimes slow. They are sometimes joyful, sometimes painful. Do not expect this trip to be one of pleasure. Joy is not the same thing as pleasure. Joy is built on love, which has for its building blocks devotion, service, and obedience. The journey is not for the purpose of your personal pleasure. Your personal well-being is watched over for the sake of your growth. Your growth is watched over for the sake of the plan. Your pleasure is irrelevant. Your joy, however, is not. Joy is the gift you receive along the way as you lift your eyes. Joy is the gift you receive each time you feel our presence with you. And joy is the gift at the end of the path. Wish for joy with all of your heart. Let pleasure come as it will, and let pleasure go with gladness.

OPHELIA on PRIDE AND FAME

Pride is a pit. Fame is the food the pitiful man feeds upon. Do not develop more of a taste for it. Its poison pervades the loss of the soul's hope. Fame is a fickle creature, loving you one moment and abandoning you the next. It is never to be relished, under any guise. See it, but be not in its court. False pride serves not God. It only hinders your journey on His path.

Fame is the pit. It is the pit into which those fall who will more for the ego than for the soul. You are no longer one of them, but you can fall into their pit as well as they can. Your bones will break as easily as theirs. Remember. And avoid what they cannot see.

OSIRIN and GUARDIAN ANGEL on FRAILTY and ACTING PITIFUL

Guardian Angel: Study love. Love is not something that you fall into quite by chance and it is not something that someone else does to you or for you. Study love. We tire of the human attitude that love comes to you. No! It comes effortlessly no more than a baby is born effortlessly. Love is like a garden, beautiful to behold in its completion but exhausting in the making. Let your self-pity dissolve into dust and be blown into the wind. Let your frustrations along the path feed your desire to learn. And study. Study!

Becca: How do I study?

Guardian Angel: The frailty of your question is the answer—be strong! Look for what is in front of you. Accept what is. Stop asking how and begin doing.

Becca (rather pitifully): How, Guardian Angel?

Osirin: Don't tease him or test him. If you must tease, tease me, and I'll answer your silly little question. First, take all of your silly little pitifulness and wrap it in a sheer gauze. Second, create an altar of love. A simple fire in your woodstove is fine. Kneel in front of the fire. Third, burn the gauze. Fourth, don't waste your time on giving up. Folks up here get mighty bored when you folks down there give up. It lacks cosmic creativity.

OSIRIN on LOVE

Of all truths of all times, the love that you are learning is the greatest. It is not love *of* anything or love *for* anything. It is objectless, goal-less, and emotionless. It is like light streaming from the sun. It is like a ray of energy, available to everyone who will see it and believe in it. Your trust in it will bring you peace and sustain your peace.

***   ***   ***   ***   ***   ***   ***

There is nothing more than love. Once you have found the pearl, then go and multiply it until you can string lovely necklaces for all of God's children.

***   ***   ***   ***   ***   ***   ***

Do not fear love. No, little one, it cannot hurt you and cannot be taken from you. Rest softly in your assurance that your love comes from us. We will never let it be depleted. We can create love from the molecules of air and light around us. People can hurt you, little one, but with our love around you, people cannot harm you.

***   ***   ***   ***   ***   ***   ***

Remember that love is not attachment, but freedom of the heart and of the spirit.

***   ***   ***   ***   ***   ***   ***

Little one, this is not a journey of ease or even of happiness. It is a journey of love. You are still young, still a child in your unfolding. Soon you will learn the key to peace. Soon you will see how easy it is to welcome your despair, to greet it at the door with a hug, to invite it in to sit by the warmth of your fire. Soon you will find that peace. But for now you must still fight against what to you feels bad, uncomfortable, or wrong. There is only one true wrong, little one, and that is turning away from love. You must choose for love. Follow love, no matter what the price. Follow love, and soon it will lead you to peace.

***   ***   ***   ***   ***   ***   ***

In how many ways can I tell you what is real? Love is real. After that sentence I must resort to metaphors. Love is a rainbow. Love is a newborn child, cradled in its parents' arms. Love is a plant, killed by the winter frosts, over which you weep. Love is an almost-blooming daffodil over which you pray with renewed hope. Love is a crystal radiating all the colors that chance upon it. Love is sitting under the full moon, asking for its blessing. Love is the pain of caring. Love is releasing all to God. Love is love.

Love is an energy. Remember that. Love to me is as tangible as your skin is to you. It is what surrounds me. It is what defines me and makes me real. You think that your skin defines you. I know that love defines me.

OSIRIN on PATIENCE

This process must take time. The ultimate lesson is far more important than how you feel today or tomorrow. Give the lesson time to grow. It will approach you soon. Wait gracefully.

***   ***   ***   ***   ***   ***   ***

No great miracle has ever unfolded immediately. For you there is only one path, one way, and you are on it. Go slowly with patience. No speeding here. No urgency. There is no need to see a miracle manifested in one day.

***   ***   ***   ***   ***   ***   ***

Let me tell you a story. Today, a story of corn. How do you know when to pick corn? The tassels tell you. You do not rip open the corn, cook it, taste it, and then discard it if it is not ready. No, you wait until nature tells you. You watch the signs. You watch the tassels. When the tassels say "pick," you pick. Then you delight in the bounty of nature. Remember— pick when ready!

***   ***   ***   ***   ***   ***   ***

These days are important, little one. Tarnish them not with impertinence or impatience. Let the quietness of the sea fill your heart. Be that quietness yourself.

We cannot talk of idle subjects now. No, we won't talk of sky and birds, of leaves and grass. Not today. We will wait beside you and with you for the moments of opening. We will wait for the time of truth and vision. We wait with you. Know clearly that we are with you. We know the quiet better than you do. Hush. Hush.

OSIRIN on FOLLOWING ONE'S OWN PATH

There is need for caution as you read of the journeys of others. And do, in love, warn others to be wary of your words.

No being can walk another's path. Suspend poetry here. Think literally. How could someone else be in your skin? How could someone else exactly replace your vibration? How could someone else exactly replace you at your son's bedside as you tuck him in? And how could someone else walk on *your* path?

This is an error in the books that you read, the error of "how-to." Do not suppose to do what someone else has done. Do not travel to Nigeria because someone else says it is wonderful, and do not avoid Quebec because someone says it is disappointing. Travel where and *wherever* you are beckoned.

The truth that lies on your path is yours. The wildflower bouquets you gather scent only your room. If they grace another's room they will be as a picture on his wall. Pictures bring softness and inspiration, but they are not alive. They bring no scent.

Pick your flowers. And encourage others to do the same. But mistake not another's bouquet as being your perfume. Confuse not another's route with your own. Do not alter your course because someone else's seems right. If your heart and soul hear God and adhere to God, then you must trust God totally. How could His highway lead you to a dead end? And how could another man's highway lead you to God?

OSIRIN on GOAL-LESS-NESS

I am closer than ever, little one, though it is hard for you to feel me.

You must let go of the belief in a goal. The idea of a goal cripples you. It makes you stumble over small pebbles that would be easily seen if you were meandering, enjoying your walk. Goals are not to be elevated onto pedestals. Listen, little one, there is no goal. Enlightenment is not a goal; it is your state of being. Meditate on that today.

There is no goal, nowhere to get to, nothing to achieve. All that you seek, no matter how great or small, is merely entertainment, diversion, or exercise along the way. It is of no consequence. Yet you must do it. That is the secret. You must do your work , you must help others, you must grow your plants, and you must write. You must do all those things, and yet those things will lead you no place that you are not right now.

Little one, remember again your father's death. Did he change? Even if you died at this moment, death would lead you nowhere that you are not right now. Relax, little one, and stop trying to reach your goal. Rest, little one. You *are* your goal.

OSIRIN on OUT-OF-BODY EXPERIENCES

Osirin: Why are you reading that book?

Becca: The one on out-of-body experiences?

Osirin: Yes. Why are you reading it?

Becca: Osirin, surely you have noticed that anybody who is anybody is jumping out of his or her skin these days.

Osirin: Why are you reading that book?

Becca: Because it intrigues me. I think it is fascinating.

Osirin: Why are you reading that book?

Becca (mellowing): For one reason. I would like to be closer to you.

Osirin: And you think being out of your body would make you closer to me?

Becca: That's what I'm thinking. Yes.

Osirin: Rubbish.

Becca (with hurt feelings): Osirin! Why would you say a thing like rubbish?

Osirin: Look it up. And do definition number 2.

Becca: Rubbish, definition number 2, means something that is worthless or nonsensical. Right after definition number 2 there's an interesting quote: "Few real masterpieces are forgotten and not much rubbish survives."

Osirin: Do you see?

Becca: Osirin, yes! At least, I think so. Let me try it myself this time.

Osirin: Fine.

Becca: You are as close as my awareness allows you to be.

Osirin: Not bad.

Becca: Osirin, I know what I was trying to say, but I don't quite understand those words that just came out of my fingers. I always understand better when you say it. Will you say it?

Osirin: Yes, little one. This time I will happily rescue you from the endless challenge of mastery. This time I will tell you simply. This time I will surround you with the softness of a pink sunrise while you absorb my words effortlessly. This is time for you to relax and to be free.

(Osirin was lulling me into hypnotic lightness with his words, with the softness of his energy, and with a definite change in the motion of my fingers on the computer keyboard.)

This is the way you know me. This is the rhythm of my fingers. See how your typing has changed. Mine is more rhythmic than yours and contains, if I may say, fewer typographical errors.

Little one, you see me everywhere. Yet you look for me in ways that I cannot appear to you. To be in those ways would be to break the laws of my physics, to break the rules of my energy. To be with you in those ways at all times would be to alter the laws of God's plan in ways that would not serve your growth. Please know and please trust. There are many ways in which I can be with you that do not change the scheme as it is. There are lovely meetings that sometimes you do not even see. I am close by. I am near. And you shall see me clearer, not as I become clearer, but as *you* become clearer. And then we will have those experiences you long for.

Being out of your body is no different, little one, from being in it. Your consciousness flows in the same river both in and out. Your soul sings to the same rhymes and rhythms both in and out. Your eyes will see to their fullest only as you are your soul, no matter whether you are in or out. Do not be enamored with being out of your body. Your body is not the enemy. Your ego is not even the enemy. It is only your blindness that holds you back. It is only lack of trust and lack of knowing. Your body is. Do not hold it in disdain. Let it be a body! And let your soul be a soul.

You will leave your body more noticeably when it is right. Meditate. Do not try and do not worry. Leaving the body is a beautiful gift at times. At other times it is a cosmic gimmick. It is not to be sought in and of itself. This, my child, is to be sought—the love of the eternal being, the peace that dwells in your soul, the everlasting light that is God. Seek nothing else, and seek *all* that is that.

A LOVE LETTER FROM OSIRIN TO BECCA

Let us rejoice. Let us lift our eyes to the nearest star. Let us fly with our hearts to its core. Let us feel the warmth and wisdom in its center. Let us celebrate our union in God's cosmos and in His total wisdom. Why be separated by time or space or centuries or planets or beliefs or illusions? We are. We are one. We are together as always and so shall be always. We fly through time like birds on wing. We soar like eagles over canyons and over the infinite Ever. Do not forget. Be ever watchful of our union and our bond. It is as always—One. Ever. Love.

OSIRIN on LIFE AND DEATH

All that you know as life is allusion. What you call birth is an allusion. It refers gently to the transition into a new dimension, the gradual and planned descent into the realm of the physical. The concept of birth is an allusion. There is no change between here and there. There is no such thing as being not alive and then being alive.

And, so, is death an allusion. There is no alteration of being. There is September first, September second, and September third. On September first you are "born," on September second you "live," and on September third you "die." And on September fourth you do more of the same, as all three are the same.

BECCA on MEDITATION

What is meditation? Meditation is a moment in which I get out of the way of my soul, allowing my soul to follow her dreams.

Meditation is a moment of recognition of my true nature—my living and loving connection with God.

Meditation is the art of quiet, a moment of no thought, no words, no needs, no motion. It is a moment of divine nothingness.

Meditation is a moment of joy—joy of being.

Meditation is a moment of seeing what is, seeing it clearly distinguished from what is not.

Meditation is a moment of a prayerful surge arising in my belly, moving into my heart, a prayer of "Wow, God! Wow!"

Meditation is a moment, a rare and special moment, when my eyes meet the eyes of another and, without words, we both see.

OSIRIN on THE PATH

You feel lost today, little one. I know. You *are* lost. So is everyone who is wise enough to look ahead and to see that the path leads nowhere. Look there. See. The path is surrounded with beautiful wildflowers, with cascading waterfalls, with birds and bees. The path at spots is paved with gold. At other spots the path is rubble and dirt. But look ahead, way ahead. The path goes nowhere. It is always just a path.

Use the analogy of the path if you wish. Follow the path if you wish. And be aware that the path leads nowhere. Paths are not to be worshipped.

OSIRIN on PEACE

Through your effort and your work, you accomplish your earthly expression of your soul's tasks and learning. But your soul itself yearns for more than your cooperation in physical expression. Your soul yearns for peace. In order for her peace to pervade your earthly being, you must do more than merely work hard. You must do more than struggle, search, and heed the teachings that you receive.

Allow peace to enter. Peace is like light streaming through a prism. If you do not pause, you may not even notice its colors. If you touch the light, nothing is there. If you listen to the light, you hear no sound. If you look at the light, you see color, but you can also see through the color. It is a mirage!

Follow the mirage. Peace, little one. Peace comes from what you do not see or touch. Peace comes from nothing that you accomplish or even from what you valiantly struggle to learn. Peace comes from your soul's rest in the warmth of God's light. Open to your soul. Feel her peace.

BECCA on DUALITY

I am me. You are you. And God is God. There you have it— that's duality. And that is the stuff of which all this trouble is made.

OSIRIN on STORING LOVE

Becca: What do I do with this love? I tried to give it away and it was not received. What do I do?

Osirin: Take the love and store it. Do not destroy it. Store it. It can save for thousands of years if properly stored. Store it as a life form, like the Thalias (my favorite daffodils). Plant something or create something. Write something. Within those vessels love is stored. Love can be stored, but you must consciously, creatively store it. That is your newest secret. What is properly stored cannot be destroyed.

OSIRIN on FEAR

Fear paves the way of destruction. In the wake of fear lie the bones of what preceded it. When you fall to fear, you fall away from all that is light. When you fall to fear, you fall away from your soul. And if there is anything greater than fear, mightier than terror, and larger than panic, it is the feeling that comes in finding yourself alone, without your soul. No person, no thing, no lifetime is greater to you than your soul. If you act as though something is greater than your soul, you are easy prey for fear.

GUARDIAN ANGEL on THE INNER VOICE

Your journey is well heeded. As you go farther, go in light. There is one more thing to do. Listen to the inner voice. Learn it. Our souls cannot be your soul. At best we are still guides. At best Jesus is still a guide. *You* are God. You will never find God *in* Jesus. You can be led to God through the God that is and is in Jesus. But you will only *know* God inside yourself. In that sense, you are deeply and truly alone. Al-one.

(I looked up "al" in the dictionary. "Al" indicates the act or process of doing or experiencing the action indicated by the verb stem. So, alone or al-one means being and experiencing the process of one-ing or oneness-ing.)

OSIRIN on THE MYSTERIES OF LIFE

Mysteries abound, little one, like stars dancing in a summer sky. Stars are not to be understood. They are for reverie, for beauty. Do not become an astronomer, consumed with a passion for dissecting the stars. Be a star gazer, a star child, a gatherer of stardust. Let the mysteries be delightfully mysterious. Giggle at them. Play in their light and dance to their music. Delight in their game of hide-and-go-seek. And labor not over them.

The mysteries hold beauty. Enjoy it. The mysteries hold music. Dance to it. And let the mysteries be mysterious! Now, go and lie under the stars.

GUARDIAN ANGEL on SEEING GOD

Drop all images of God. Drop all understandings. Let God be who God is. Then and only then can you discover Him. The One Whom you seek cannot penetrate the rigid walls of your mind's false expectations. Drop them. Stand in a chasm of nothingness. Only then will you see Him.

OSIRIN on ONENESS

Look at that tree. See the limbs of that great oak reaching a hundred feet into the sky. And look now at that leaf—that one farthest out on the farthest branch of the farthest limb. Look closely at that leaf.

That leaf is no less a part of the tree than is the leaf that snuggles close to the main trunk. The farthest leaf is no less a vital, living part of the tree. But see how far it is from the trunk. See how far it is from the roots of the tree.

Do you think that leaf knows who it is? Do you think it recognizes that it is intimately attached to the grand oak? Do you think it is comforted by the knowledge of the part it plays with the oak?

Or do you imagine, being so very far out into the air, it thinks it exists alone? Do you think the leaf prides itself in its independence? Do you imagine it considers itself unique, individual, and special?

If the leaf wishes to taste the true meaning of individuality, then let it catch a high wind, be ripped from the tree, and fall to the ground.

OSIRIN on THE EGO

Becca: Osirin, I cannot remain in a formless form all the time. I cannot be in a human body and be mindless, thoughtless, and characterless 24 hours a day. I don't like coming back into my personality very much, but I don't see an alternative for now. Teach me. Teach me what this all means. How can I be my soul and be running around in a body at the same time? What is the goal? What is possible?

Osirin, I want to live longer in this world. I want to serve. I don't want to go meditate in Tibet for the rest of my earth years, but I don't want to be a prisoner of my earthbound personality and ego either. I want to be God-ness, and I want to be God-ness now. I don't want to wait until I die, and I don't want to have to die now in order to be God-ness. Such a dilemma. And, Osirin, there are no teachers around here. I have no teachers. Help!

Osirin: And why do you think I was sent to teach you? There are teachers around, others who are striving to be God. Your eyes will find them soon.

The worship of one's own ego—that is the problem here. You had to struggle very hard in this lifetime to build a strong and robust ego. You worked against strong odds—social odds, psychological odds, and spiritual odds. And you developed an ego of strength and power. Now you must be very cautious in your relationship with that ego. It is not you.

Becca: Then why did I need to develop it?

Osirin: Without it you could not do your work in this world. With it, however, you must struggle for perspective. You sculpted a thing of power, strength, and beauty. You created this rather impressive statue through years and years of work. It is quite good. Now, be careful that you do not worship it. It is a statue. It has no life. *No life.* It is merely a decoration. Hear me, your personality, your ego, and all that you usually think of when you use the word "I" is *dead.* There is no life there. It is dead. It is a stone statue created to decorate your home.

Think of your "I" as being like furniture. The furniture in your home is not wrong or bad. Its purpose is to provide some support for those who live in the house. But the furniture itself is not alive and is hardly worshipped. If it all burned in a fire, the lives of those who lived in the house would be minimally changed. The furniture is for helping to perform tasks of sitting, lying, writing, and eating. The furniture is useful, but that is all. And it is the same with your "I"—useful if used, destructive if worshipped.

BECCA'S INNER JESUS on WHO HE IS

Do not limit me by your thoughts. You see a bird flying and you compare me to the bird in its grace and freedom. And then you limit me. I am the bird, the flock of birds, and the sky through which they fly.

Do not limit me in your thoughts. You think of me as kind, so you doubt my harshness. You think of me as sober and you doubt my joy. You miss me often because of the limitations you impose.

You think of me as love. You do not yet see the love that hides in your pain, so you miss me in the throes of your pain. You think of me as light, and you miss the flicker that lives in the pit of your darkness.

I am not limited. When you see that is so, your eyes will grow a thousand times their present size.

JOSHUA ZINN (age 4) on
THE MEANING OF LIFE

Mommy and Daddy, do you know what is important in life? In everybody's life? The sun, the moon, the stars, love, energy, darkness, rain, winter, fall, God, and Jesus. That's what.

JOSHUA (age 4) on THE SOUL

Becca: Josh, I have something important to tell you.
Josh (playing wildly with a toy motorcycle): OK, tell me.
Becca: Look into my eyes and I'll tell you.
Josh (too busy to be bothered): I don't have to look in your eyes.
Becca: This is important. Besides, can you tell what is in my eyes without looking?
Josh: Yes.
Becca: OK, wise guy. What is in my eyes right now?
Josh (still looking away and playing): Your soul.

JOSHUA (age 4) on
LOVE MESSAGES FROM GOD

During the day I had been feeling quite melancholy while digging in my garden when the following thought entered my mind with sudden intensity: If I were to die at this moment, what would God think was my main accomplishment on earth?

I thought to myself that I have tried to create some love and beauty on the earth. As I was digging in the earth to plant yet another tree, I felt that perhaps I had been more successful in creating beauty through my gardens than I had been in creating love. I did not mention any of these thoughts to Josh.

In the evening as Josh and I were cuddling before bed, we had this conversation:

Becca: Josh, you know that special night light I brought into your room? I think I'll let you keep it here if you are very careful with it.

Josh: Good. Do you know how long I want to keep it here?

Becca: How long?

Josh: Until God decides it is time for me to die.

Becca: Well, be very careful with it and it will be beautiful in your room for a very long time.

Josh: Mom, do you know what is important?

Becca: What?

Josh: God and Jesus.

Becca: Can you see God and Jesus in your mind?

Josh: Yes.

Becca: Let's close our eyes and see them.

Josh: OK.

Becca: What do God and Jesus look like and feel like to you?

Josh: Jesus has a moustache and a long beard. (pause) And green toes!

Becca: No, serious. How does he seem to you?

Josh: Serious? He seems very nice.

Becca: And what about God?

Josh: He looks like Jesus. Just like Jesus.

Becca: And do they say anything to you?

Josh: I can't hear anything yet.

Becca: You can't hear them through your ears, you know.

Josh: I know. Sometimes God tells me secrets in my mind.

Becca: Listen now.

Josh: He said something to me.

Becca: What did he say?

Josh: He said, "I hope your mommy enjoys her flowers."

JOSHUA (age 4) on LOVE

Josh: Mom, why do you always make jokes about things?
Becca: Oh, because life is kind of funny.
Josh: What else?
Becca: Well, life is also a challenge.
Josh (in grand theatrical style): Yes, and life is *hard*!
Becca: Yes, life is hard! So, life is funny and challenging and hard. But those are not the most important things about life. Do you know the meaning of life?
Josh: Yep.
Becca: What is it?
Josh (casually): Love.

JOSHUA (age 5) on ONENESS

Josh: Mommy, why did you tell that little girl in the grocery store that she had nice ribbons in her hair?
Becca: That was a special moment, Josh. She and I kept looking at each other. I could tell she liked me, and she knew I liked her. So, telling her she had nice ribbons was sort of a secret way of saying, "I like you."
Josh: How do you know she likes you?
Becca: I could just tell.
Josh (in a sassy voice): Oh, yeah? Are you her?
Becca: No. But I could just tell.
Josh (still sassy): Well, then, I'm you and I know everything you're thinking. (Mellowing) You know, actually God made everybody the same.
Becca: What do you mean?
Josh: I am everybody in the world in a way.
Becca: Wow! That's a very smart thing to say, Josh. Can you say more about what you mean?
Josh (after thinking for a few moments): Mommy, all people have the very same heart in a way.

JOSHUA (age 6) on LOVE

Becca (picking up Josh from kindergarten on Valentine's Day): I have something very serious to tell you, Josh. It's very very very important.

Josh: Well, what is it?

Becca: You have to listen carefully because this is really serious. Are you ready?

Josh: Come on, Mom. Tell me!

Becca: OK, here goes. I . . . LOVE . . . YOU!

Josh: I know. Everybody loves everybody on Valentine's Day.

Becca: That's right. What does love mean to you, Josh?

Josh: Love is love. That's what is means.

Becca (with histrionic flair): True, my dear. But what is the deep philosophical and spiritual reality underlying love?

Josh: Well, Mom, I'll tell you this. If there was no love, there would be no humans, all the stars would be unhappy, and God would be too sad to make the world.

Becca: I love you a bunch, sugar. Happy Valentine's Day.

POSTSCRIPT

"To learn to talk with angels
is really a way of learning
to talk with ourselves
and with each other
in new and profoundly
deeper ways."

(quoted with permission from *To Hear the Angels Sing* by Dorothy MacLean, 1980. Lorian Press, PO Box 663, Issaquah, WA, 98027).

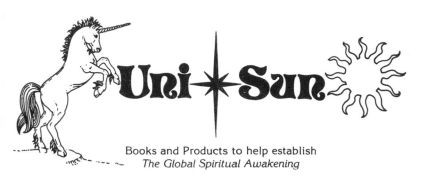

Books and Products to help establish
The Global Spiritual Awakening

Becca Zinn is a bright new star in UNI★SUN's constellation of channeled writers. Her unique talents and insights will soon be applied to the production of another book, hopefully we can have it ready in 1987.

We at UNI★SUN are happy and proud to publish books and offer products that make a real contribution to the global spiritual awakening that has already begun on this planet. Becca Zinn is one of several important new authors whose works we publish. Please write for our free catalogue.

UNI★SUN
P. O. Box 25421
Kansas City, Missouri 64119
U.S.A.